The Put 'em Up! Preserving Answer Book

The

Put 'em Up!

PRESERVING

ANSWER BOOK

399 Solutions to All Your Questions
Canning • Freezing • Drying
Fermenting • Making Infusions

SHERRI BROOKS VINTON

best-selling author of *Put 'em Up!* and *Put 'em Up! Fruit*

Storey Publishing

The mission of Storey Publishing is to serve our customers by publishing practical information that encourages personal independence in harmony with the environment.

Edited by Margaret Sutherland and Molly Jackel
Art direction by Mary Winkelman Velgos
Text production by Liseann Karandisecky

Cover photography by Mars Vilaubi, author photo by Chris Bartlett
Illustrations by © Elara Tanguy

Indexed by Nancy D. Wood

Be sure to read all the instructions thoroughly before undertaking any of the techniques or recipes in this book and follow all of the recommended safety guidelines.

Storey Publishing
210 MASS MoCA Way
North Adams, MA 01247
www.storey.com

Printed in China by Shenzhen Caimei Printing Co., Ltd.
10 9 8 7 6 5 4 3 2 1

Library of Congress Cataloging-in-Publication Data on file

Storey Publishing is committed to making environmentally responsible manufacturing decisions. This book was printed on paper made from sustainably harvested fiber.

*For all the eaters who ask questions
and demand answers*

Acknowledgments

I would like to thank my husband, Drew, and my kids, Ava and Thayer, for their constant support, lack of fussiness when I travel for weeks on end, and general buena onda. How lucky I am.

Thanks Mom, Granny Toni, and Gran for my formative eating years. I owe each of you for my obsession with all things edible.

I would like to thank Lisa Ekus and The Lisa Ekus Group for their kind attention and dedication to the movement.

I greatly appreciate Storey Publishing for signing this hat trick of three books. It has been a fabulous project and I appreciate everyone who contributed to the success of the series particularly my wonderful, even-keeled, calm, and inspiring editor, Margaret Sutherland, and the tireless, supportive, ever-smiling publicist, Alee Moncy. What a team!

I'd like to give a shout out to my kitchen sistahs (and bros) who share the passion for delicious, homemade food and dedicate themselves to teaching others how to feed themselves.

And thank you readers, eaters, canners, and cooks everywhere for your support of local farmers and real, good food. Now get in there and cook up something tasty!

Contents

PART 3: *Putting Your Skills to Work*

Introduction

Is there any home cooking activity that churns up more anxiety than food preservation? Roasting your first Thanksgiving Day bird, perhaps. I understand that the turkey hotline rings off the hook on that day. Since *Put 'em Up!* first came out, in 2010, my phone and e-mail have been getting their share of jingles as well. Eaters all across the country have reached out with their preserving questions, concerns, and triumphs. The Q & A sessions in my classes have been terrifically robust. There is so much to know about this craft, and it has been a challenge and a pleasure to work through the answers to all of the questions that have been posed along the way.

This book is by no means an exhaustive overview of all food preservation processes. It does, however, aim to answer the most frequently asked questions about putting up your own produce. Consider it a hit list of the problems and solutions that many home preservers face when drying, freezing, fermenting, infusing, and canning their food.

I am very grateful to the eaters who have trusted me to help them clear their kitchen hurdles. I hope, in some small way, that I have encouraged more people to return to the kitchen to cook up, preserve, and enjoy not only great-tasting food but also lasting memories of lovely times and delicious things shared with friends and family. After all, while there is a great deal of technical information involved in these processes, the goal isn't to perform a science experiment. It's to create your next great meal.

I hope you find the answers here to all of your preserving questions. But if you don't, give me a shout. The hotline's always open.

PART 1

Getting Started

*I*f you were to ask me the hardest thing about preserving your own food, I would have to say it's simply getting started. For many home cooks, taking their first turn at preservation can be intimidating. Learning to use unfamiliar tools and mastering the techniques seems too high a hurdle to clear. Even the most experienced home preservers can find themselves procrastinating before jumping into the season's first canning session as they tick through a mental list of equipment and ingredients they need to gather.

But preserving your own food doesn't have to be difficult or frustrating. "Getting Started" gives you all the tips, tricks, and information you need to slip right into the preserving pool. Whether you are looking to dip a toe in and test the waters — perhaps by simply drying a bit of fruit or freezing a batch of berries — or you are ready to jump head first into putting up your summer garden, this section gives you all the fundamental knowledge you need to get on your way.

CHAPTER 1

Basics

Walk through the aisles of any grocery store and you are sure to find shelves so heavily stocked, it seems easy to argue against preserving your own food. We can get anything at any time these days. But it's important not to mistake quantity for quality. The best food still comes out of your kitchen, from your hands. You can make food that tastes better, that *is* better, than anything you can find in the store. It is easier than you think, and safer than you've heard. And you're sure to come across recipes that allow you to create things that are more fantastically flavorful than anything money could buy.

Why Preserve?

Q What's to love about preserving your own food?

A Oh, let me count the ways! For me, it's all about connection. Preserving my own food keeps me connected to my local farms during the fallow season. It just plain feels good to see food from the people I know and trust lined up on my shelves. It also connects me to my past as I resurrect the tastes and techniques that have been passed down through generations of my family and other preservers like me. And preserving food connects me to my friends and family. Sometimes we are all working together in the kitchen to put food up, and that feels great. I am also able to bring jars of my tasty preserved foods to friends when I visit or send them care packages across the miles. It's a way to feed some of the people I wish I could have around my table more often. Maybe that's a little sentimental, but food's pretty deep that way for me. Here are a few reasons I would recommend that you give it a whirl:

- **Delicious.** Homemade food always tastes best. There isn't an assembly line out there that can compete with a good turn in a home kitchen.

- **No preservatives.** You control what goes in the jar.

- **Preserves local agriculture.** Canning is just another way to buy and eat local.
- **Uses up surplus.** Waste not, want not.
- **Fun.** Spending time with good food and maybe even some friends and family to help out — what could be better?

Q Can you really preserve your own food if you have a modern (read: busy) schedule?

A No doubt about it, preserving food takes time. But it doesn't always have to be a lot of time. There are projects that can be accomplished in a jiffy. While you might not always have the chunk of time you want to put up a year's worth of tomatoes, there are other preserving methods at your fingertips that can help you keep your pantry stocked. Here are a few quick preserving ideas for when you have more produce than time:

- **Freeze it.** Frozen fruits, such as berries, can be added directly to recipes without defrosting. You can also save up your berries and turn them into sweet spreads and more, later in the season.

- **Dry it.** Ten minutes is all it takes to run a piece of thick string through the stems of a couple pounds of chile peppers. Let them dry, and you will have spice all year long.

- **Chill it.** Vegetables such as cucumbers, carrots, turnips, kohlrabi, radishes, and zucchini make terrific refrigerator pickles. Submerge them under your favorite brine and they will keep in the fridge for at least 3 weeks.

> ## Kitchen Tip
>
> Enlist reinforcements! It's super to have help when you are preserving your food. Even kids can pitch in, particularly with the prep — they are great at pitting cherries, peeling tomatoes, and skinning grapes. Getting help — even from the little ones — means your home food preservation will be fast and fun.

Q I've never been a gardener. Is home food preservation for me?

A That makes two of us! I have never had a green thumb, yet I put up loads of food. I source everything from local growers by either visiting them at their farms, shopping at the farmers' market, or going to the U-pick. And I am happy to say that when my gardening friends find themselves flush, they know that I have a will-can-for-food policy that will keep us both well fed.

Some farmers will offer a discount if you buy in bulk — by the bushel, case, or flat. If that sounds like too much for you, get together with some friends and put in an order together. It helps the grower move product, and it can make your grocery bill a little lighter.

Q Why does preserving continue to be popular?

A Preserving food is by no means a modern invention; it's how eaters smooth out an erratic food supply and has been practiced pretty much since humans began to eat. Methods of food preservation, having originated largely from the environmental conditions of the area, are numerous and varied across cultures. In cold climates, food was frozen, while in arid regions, food was dried.

Even today, a trip to a desert bazaar will still offer you an array of dried fruits that have soaked up the sun. In fact, drying food is one of the oldest food preservation techniques. It allowed nomadic tribes to preserve foods that would spoil and it made the food lighter so that it could be transported more easily.

Eaters also relied on "controlled rot" to work with the natural bacteria in their area to help them preserve food. Beer, one of the first recipes ever written, is the delightful result of preserving grain through fermentation. Wine, cheese, yogurt, and pickles are all aged foods suspended in a delicious state by the beneficial effects of bacteria on foodstuffs.

While canning as we know it relies on the modern invention of the three-piece jar, jarring and potting foods under a layer of oil or fat is the same concept of airtight food storage and a tradition that reaches back through the ages.

So the next time someone sniffs at preserving as a passing fancy, know that you aren't just being cool, but that you are also continuing an ancient food tradition.

Safety

Q What are the most common causes of food contamination?

A Contamination is a risk anytime you are preparing food. Preserving is no exception. Follow these easy tips for reliable, delicious results:

- **Follow your recipe.** Can't say it enough. This is not the time for improvisation. Stick to the script to maintain the necessary acid balance that makes food preservation safe.

- **Keep your work space clean and organized.** You don't have to sterilize your kitchen, but be sure that you give everything a good wash-down before you start.

- **Keep your food clean.** Wash off all visible dirt, give sturdy foods a good scrub, and rinse all delicate items in several changes of water before you bring your food to the cutting board.

- **Check your jars.** Make sure the lips are smooth, with no hairline cracks in the glass that can lead to seal failure or breakage down the line.

- **Use only fresh food.** If it isn't good enough to eat, it isn't good enough to preserve.

- **Did I say to follow your recipe?**

Q Do I need to use any special sanitizers on my kitchen surfaces and equipment before I start preserving food?

A When preserving your own food, you will get the best results when your work space is clean and organized. Home kitchens, however, can never be completely sterile, and you shouldn't worry about trying to get them hospital clean. You don't need to swab your counters down with alcohol, bleach, or any other harsh chemicals. Just wash equipment such as tongs, ladles, and pots in hot, soapy water, and wipe counters down before you begin.

When I am using the boiling-water method, I also like to lay out a clean tea towel. It not only gives me a fresh work surface, but it also catches the drips from this wet process. An apron is a nice idea, too, but not necessary. It's a good idea to tie back long hair to keep strays from making their way into your recipes.

You don't have to presterilize your equipment for any recipe processed for 10 minutes or longer. However, if your filled jars will spend less than 10 minutes in the boiling-water bath, then everything that touches your food — jars and all equipment — must be presterilized by submerging everything in boiling water for 10 minutes.

Q What is botulism and what causes it?

A Botulism, the "big B" of canning, is the illness caused by *Clostridium botulinum* bacteria that can sicken those who are exposed to it and can, in some cases, be fatal. The bacteria are very common; they are often found in soil and can be present in untreated water. However, the bacteria need to be in a low-acid, anaerobic environment to produce the illness-inducing toxin. While one can create these conditions in a canning jar, you have to veer very far off course to do so.

If you follow these golden rules of canning, you can feel confident that your canned foods will be delicious and wholesome:

Follow your recipe. Never alter the ratios of produce to acid in your recipe; this will raise the pH to a level that may be unsafe for your preserving method. Process only high-acid recipes with the boiling-water method (see page 95). Process nonacidic foods (such as vegetables without added acid, meats, and fish) using a pressure canner (see page 122).

Never try to cheat the clock. Process foods for the time indicated in your recipe. Adjust for altitude. Dry foods for the amount of time indicated, and do so slowly and thoroughly to avoid creating airtight but moisture-filled food, which can become contaminated.

Kitchen Tip

Hold the phone! Or at least make sure you're on speaker. Once you start a home food preservation project, you should move through the process smoothly, without interruptions that will make you start and stop. No stopping to take a call or run an errand. You don't need to rush through it, but keep a steady pace for the best results.

Q How can I tell if my food is contaminated?

A If you are following your recipe, there is very little chance that you will run into problems. While not all contamination is apparent, there are some signs to look out for. In the off chance that you see any of these warning signs, dispose of your food immediately:

- Mold in a sealed jar. While ferments may have some mold that forms on top and can be disposed of, mold inside a sealed jar is not okay.
- Fizzing or bubbling inside a jar of processed food.
- Musty or boozy smells inside a sealed jar.
- Color changes beyond a small amount of dulling or darkening in a low-sugar spread.
- Slimy textures.

Q I have a collection of preserving recipes passed down from my family. Can I use those?

A I would never pull anyone away from family traditions. There is a lot of nuance in preserving food that can't always be captured in a book, and a lot of solid, tested knowledge that has been passed down for generations. If you and your family have been using a certain recipe or technique that has proven reliable and delicious for you, that's great.

However, many techniques, such as open-kettle canning, have been put aside to make way for more reliable methods with safer, more predictable results. I suggest you give these modern methods some thought and see if you don't agree that they allow for a greater rate of success.

If you have a recipe that is dear to you and you want to make sure it is safe, you might consider approaching your local ag extension office (cooperative agricultural extension service) to have them review it. They might give the thumbs-up or offer a simple tweak or bit of advice that can give you more consistent results. Samples can also be sent off to food labs for testing.

If you are just starting out, I suggest you avail yourself of the many modern preserving books that have hit the shelves in the past few years. We are always learning new ideas for making time spent preserving food more efficient and results more predictable.

Learn the Lingo

The names of homemade preserves, like *jam* and *jelly*, get thrown around all the time, particularly on restaurant menus, where they are treated with a nice dose of poetic license. The fact is, the terms cannot be used interchangeably; each has a distinct definition that describes its ingredients and preparation method. Here are some of the most common terms used for home-preserved items.

Chutney. In flavor, chutneys lie somewhere between preserves and pickles; even though they are often made with fruit as their main ingredient, they utilize vinegar for its preserving power. Chutneys are made with all kinds of fruits simmered with spices and savory flavorings, such as garlic and onions. Some common ones include mango, tamarind, cilantro, and onion chutneys.

Compote. Contains large pieces of fresh or dried fruit gently simmered in sugar syrup. In a compote, care is taken to maintain the shape of the pieces so that they remain intact and suspended in a clear liquid. The syrup can be a simple combination of water and sugar, or it can be flavored to enhance the taste of the fruit.

Conserve. A thick fruit mixture cooked gently in sugar syrup so that large pieces of fruit remain, resulting in a texture that has fewer whole fruit pieces than a compote but is a bit chunkier than a preserve. Raisins or nuts are frequently added to conserves.

Curd. A sweet, creamy spread made with eggs, butter, and citrus juice. Curds can be a challenge to master, as they require precise attention to the quality of ingredients, cooking times, and temperatures. Although the most popular flavor is lemon, lime and orange curds are equally delicious.

Fruit Cheese. A paste made of fruit, lemon juice, and sugar that has been cooked down to a very dense texture. When cooled, fruit cheese should be firm enough to slice with a knife.

Gastrique. A pungent vinegar-based sauce that is heavily reduced to take on a thick, syrupy texture. The base of the gastrique is a combination of vinegar and caramelized sugar that is cooked down and used as a canvas for a featured flavoring, such as berries or citrus juice. Because of their intense flavors, gastriques are used in small amounts to accent the flavor of dishes.

Infusion. A liquid, typically vinegar or a high-alcohol spirit, that has taken on the flavor of a featured fruit, vegetable, spice, or herb. The flavoring agent is submerged in the base liquid and allowed to steep until it has infused the liquid with flavor.

Jam. A sweet spread made with mashed fruit or fruit that has been cooked until it has fallen apart. Jams rely on either naturally occuring or added pectin to achieve a gelled consistency thick enough that a spoonful will hold its shape.

Jelly. A sweet, clear spread made from fruit juice alone. Jelly's texture is firmer than that of a jam but not as firm as that of a fruit cheese or paste.

Ketchup. What makes ketchup, ketchup? In my view, it's the familiar combination of flavors and spices that support the fruit in the form of a smooth, pourable sauce. While we most often associate ketchup with tomatoes, other fruits, used with a similar range of spices as found in the typical version, can offer subtle twists on this familiar condiment.

Leather. Typically made out of fruit, leathers are dried sheets of puréed produce. The purée may be lightly sweetened before it is spread out on a flat surface to dehydrate. Leathers are typically eaten as snacks but can be used in recipes that call for dried fruit.

Liqueur. A sweetened spirit infusion. Liqueur is often potent and, as such, is served in small amounts, typically after a meal.

Marmalade. A thick spread made from seeded citrus fruit. The peel, which is sliced thinly, minced, or shredded, is a necessary element, bringing both texture and flavor to the spread. Because of the high pectin level of citrus fruits, marmalades can be made without added thickeners. Simply sugar and fruit cooked down to a gel will give a lively marmalade.

Pickle. A fruit or vegetable that has been acidified to prolong its shelf life. Two kinds of pickles are featured in this book. Vinegar pickles, such as Bread-and-Butter Chips (page 78), use bottled vinegar to help cure the fruit. Lacto-fermented pickles, such as Classic Fermented Sauerkraut (page 162), are submerged in a salt solution and allowed to ferment, creating the lactic acid that preserves them.

Preserve. The word *preserve* is often used to describe any fruit that has been cured to protect its flavor and texture. However, it does have a specific definition: fruit that has been cooked into a thick spread, with large pieces suspended in a gelled syrup.

Purée. A slightly thickened sauce that has been mashed or blended to a smooth consistency.

Relish. A slightly sweet but tangy condiment made of fruits or vegetables. Relishes contain uniformly cut pieces that retain their shape and texture when cooked.

Salsa. The Spanish word for "sauce." Although we may think of salsa only as a red dip for tortilla chips, the term actually applies to a wide range of piquant sauces that can be smooth or quite chunky and are made from both fruits and vegetables.

Vinegar. A fermented liquid; natural bacteria have acted on these liquids, such as wine or apple juice, to digest their natural sugars and convert them into acetic acid. Any fruit juice can be converted into vinegar as long as the beneficial bacteria are allowed to propagate in an aerobic environment.

CHAPTER 2

Sourcing and Storage

There is no preservation method that will improve the quality of your food. You have to start with delicious, wholesome goods to get tasty results. Here are some thoughts on finding the good stuff and keeping it that way.

Finding Good Food

Q Where is the best place to get your produce?

A Locally sourced foods are the best candidates for home food preservation. Here is why you want produce that comes from your local grower, farmers' market, or backyard garden:

- **It's fresh.** Freshness is important to the process. Locally grown foods have made the shortest trip from the field to you. You want to put up food that has been harvested no more than a day before you preserve it. It will have the best flavor and also will not have had a chance to decay and build up a bacterial load that can overwhelm the preserving process.

- **It's clean.** Food that you buy directly from the grower or that you harvest yourself will also be less likely to have been treated with the waxes and fungicides that are often applied to supermarket produce to prolong its shelf life. Such treatments can prevent the absorption of brines and syrups used in the preservation process and interfere with your results.

- **It's green.** The impact of toxic applications can be magnified during preserving, particularly in foods that are dehydrated. When you are buying directly from the grower or growing the food yourself, it's easier to find organic or minimally sprayed produce.

- **It keeps agriculture in our culture.** Wendell Berry said it best. To paraphrase, a decentralized food chain is the most stable and reliable system of agriculture. Food shouldn't be something that is "grown over there." It should be something that is grown everywhere so that everyone has a chance to know their farmer and connect with the source of their dinner.

Q I saw some fruit called "seconds" for sale. Is this good produce for preserving?

A Food meant for preserving should be wholesome and as fresh as possible. *Seconds* can be defined very differently and indicate a range of imperfection. So it's important to categorize the produce more specifically to judge whether it would be safe for preserving.

If the seconds are just less pretty versions of good fruit — they are a bit misshapen or smaller than usual, or have some discoloration or superficial imperfections — they are fine to preserve with any method.

However, any produce that has had its skin or peel compromised — by insect damage, small areas of rot, or a small amount of bruising or puncture, for example — is not recommended for canning. Such damage could have introduced more bacteria into the food than the process can handle. A spot of mold, for instance, is like the tip of an iceberg — the black area you see is just the top of tendrils of contamination that reach deep into the fruit. Freezing is the better method for preserving these kinds of seconds that have limited areas of damage. Just trim the offending parts of the product away.

Food that is very withered or rotting should be composted, not preserved, as no amount of curing, fermenting, or freezing will ever improve it.

Q They're running a special on cucumbers at the local grocery. Are those good for preserving?

A All food that is destined for canning or fermenting should be at its absolute freshest — picked no more than a day before processing — but cucumbers are particularly sensitive to waiting for their date with the canner. Cucumbers that are too long on

Kitchen Tip

Buy or pick your produce as close to preserving time as possible — the same day would be preferable, or no more than a day ahead. Old produce won't perform as well and picks up bacteria over time that can lead to less-than-satisfactory results.

the vine will often have hollow centers and a bitter taste that is less than ideal for pickle making. Those that have seen too much time from harvest to pot can take on a withered appearance. And last, cucumbers, like much of the produce in the market, are often heavily waxed to extend their shelf life; such coatings can interfere with the brine's ability to penetrate the fruit. For best results, pickle young, fresh, unwaxed cucumbers that are harvested close to home.

Q Don't I need bushels of produce for preserving?

A I have to say that when I get all set up to preserve, I like to really get in there and put up a lot — a preserving marathon is a good day for me. But not everyone views an extended session in the kitchen as joyfully as I do, and you needn't clear your day to get a good amount done. Some recipes, such as quick jams and jellies (see Quick Blueberry Jam, page 182), come together so rapidly you can be in and out of the kitchen in just a little more time than it takes to bring your canner to a boil. Ketchups and chutneys require a little prep time up front but then can simmer away while you cook dinner.

There are a few endeavors, however, that one would consider to be more of a project. Canning a case of whole tomatoes, for example, can take about 3 hours from start to finish when you add up the coring, peeling, and lengthy processing time. For these extended projects, I take the "in for a penny, in for a pound" approach and line up multiple batches in succession. That way, while one batch is processing, the other is being prepped. Using this approach and having a few friends over to keep me company — and maybe help out, too — makes the canning session much more productive (and a hoot!).

Q I was gifted a large box of citrus for the holidays and want to use it to make marmalade, but I think it might be waxed. Can I still use it?

A Much of the produce sold at the retail level is waxed to make it last longer on the shelf or in transit. It's best to avoid waxed fruits. But if you cannot, it's important to remove as much of the wax as possible before proceeding with your recipe to maximize the penetration of any brines or syrups. To do so, fill a large bowl with very hot tap water (do not use boiling water, which will remove the essential oils from the fruit), add your fruit, and let it soak for a few minutes. Then scrub it thoroughly (but not so aggressively that you start to scratch away the zest) with a vegetable brush and unscented dish soap. Rinse thoroughly and proceed with your recipe.

Q Citrus is not local to me, but I want to make some preserved lemons and maybe some curd. Are there any reliable sources for citrus?

A There are some lovely, independently owned orchards that sell unwaxed, untreated fruit directly to consumers. Supporting these businesses is a great way to get wonderful produce and keep such operations running. You can use the website www.localharvest.org to find one that meets your needs.

Q What is heirloom produce?

A Heirloom seeds reproduce "true," meaning that unlike more common hybrid seeds, you can plant the seeds saved from such produce and get the same variety again; plant a seed from an heirloom Mortgage Lifter tomato and you will get a Mortgage Lifter tomato off the resulting vine. They are called heirloom seeds because they have been passed down from seed to plant to seed again through generations. Heirloom produce is prized for its flavor and unique growing characteristics. For example, some varieties do better in wet climates; others are suited to drier conditions. You can find a wide range of colors and flavors among the different heirloom varieties of a particular heirloom fruit or vegetable and different cooking qualities as well. Some heirloom apple varieties, for example, are best for storage, others for cooking, and others for eating out of hand. Some heirloom

Kitchen Tip

I love to can heirloom tomatoes and enjoy the wide range of colors that these special varieties offer. When adding them to blended sauces and salsas, I try to stick with colors that go together so that my end result has an appealing hue. Reds, yellows, and oranges work well together. Yellows, greens, and whites are another good combination.

varieties of tomato are best for sauce making and canning; others are prized as good slicers.

Unlike commercial varieties, which are grown for their uniformity and ability to endure extended transport, heirlooms are valued for their terrific flavor. Because of their great taste, heirloom varieties have become increasingly popular. You can find heirloom varieties of all kinds of produce — Dragon's Tongue beans, Romanesco broccoli, Golden Hubbard squash, and more — at your local farmers' market or farm stand. Or grow your own!

Q My farmers' market has all kinds of carrots — red, white, yellow — can I use these in my canning recipes?

A You can use any kind of carrots interchangeably. Red, white, yellow — they all cook up pretty consistently. Just be sure to cut your produce to the size indicated in the recipes. Keep in mind that deeply colored carrots will lose their color during processing and may tinge any other produce in the jar. A few red carrots in a jar of pickles, for example, will color their neighbors pink. You'll lose the color in the carrots, but it makes for a very pretty brine. Nothing like seeing the world through rose-colored pickles!

Q What is the difference between fresh dill and dill weed?

A The dill plant has several components that have different applications. Dill weed is the feathery, deep green leaf of the dill plant. Dill seed is the seed of the plant, which can be harvested after the plant is mature. A head of dill is the umbrella-shaped flower of the plant after it has gone to seed.

You can find all of these parts of the dill plant in pickling

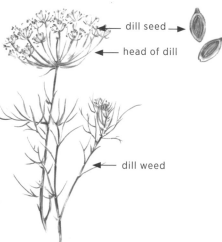

dill seed

head of dill

dill weed

recipes. Keep in mind that the leaves have the most delicate flavor and the seeds the strongest.

Q Can I use golden beets instead of red in my recipes?

A You can absolutely swap out red beets for golden beets or even candy cane (Chioggia) beets if you can find them. The color is irrelevant to your recipe (but will look gorgeous in your jar). Candy canes will lose their stripes during cooking but will taste just as fine.

Q Can I use white peaches in my recipes?

A White peaches have less acid than yellow peaches, so they will raise the pH of your recipe. This may not be significant if you are working with a heavily acidified recipe, such as a salsa. But be careful when canning white peaches whole or in recipes that have only a dash of acid, such as jams (see recipe, page 26) and jellies. The difference may be enough to throw off your acid balance and present a problem. White peaches also have a more delicate texture that does not stand up to heat very well — fine in a sauce or jam, but not a great whole-fruit option. For best results, stick to canning recipes developed specifically for white peaches.

Q Do blueberries have seeds?

A Yes, blueberries have tiny, soft seeds. They are edible and you needn't try to remove them for your recipe. If you are averse to the somewhat gritty texture that blueberry seeds can lend to jams, you can strain the fruit for blueberry jelly.

Q What are yellow wax beans? Can I use them in my recipes?

A Yellow wax beans are identical to the more typical

Kitchen Tip

Cheesecloth is frequently used in home food preservation techniques — to drain fruit for jelly and to cover infusions and ferments, for example. If you are buying the material in the paltry 2- to 3-yard lengths sold in the grocery, you can really go through a lot and the cost can start to add up. You can often substitute an unbleached, untreated muslin fabric, if the weave is loose enough. Check your local fabric store for availability or purchase online by the bolt for even greater savings.

WHITE PEACH JAM

Makes about 7 cups

White peaches have a lovely, floral scent and flavor that sets them apart from the more common (but still delicious!) yellow peaches that you often find at the market. White peaches are also less acidic than yellow peaches, which gives them a delicate flavor when eaten out of hand. It also means, however, that you have to add an extra boost of acid, in the form of lemon juice as I've done here, to keep them safe in the jar. Follow this recipe to white peach perfection.

INGREDIENTS

    1 gallon plus 1 cup water
  ½ cup bottled lemon juice
    1 quart ice cubes
    5 pounds white peaches
    5 cups sugar

PREPARE

1. Combine 1 cup of the water and ¼ cup of the lemon juice in a large heavy-bottomed pot and set aside. Combine the remaining 1 gallon of water and the ice in a large bowl, cooler, or your impeccably clean kitchen sink.

2. Bring a large pot of water to a boil. Working in batches, blanch the fruit, 1 pound at a time, by dropping it in the boiling water for 30 seconds to loosen the skins. Scoop out the peaches from the water and plunge them into the prepared ice-water bath. Repeat with the remaining fruit. Drain.

3. Peel, pit, and chop the peaches, adding them directly to the lemon juice mixture as you go. Slowly bring to a boil, stirring constantly to avoid scorching. Reduce heat and simmer 15 to 20 minutes, mashing as necessary to get a smooth texture, until the fruit is softened and falling apart. Add the sugar and the remaining ¼ cup of lemon juice and cook until the gel stage is reached, about 25 minutes (see Getting a Good Set, page 199).

PRESERVE

Refrigerate: Ladle into 8-ounce jars, leaving ¼ inch of headspace between the top of the jam and the top of the jar. Jam keeps covered for up to 3 weeks.

Can: Use the boiling-water method (see page 95). Ladle the jam into clean, hot 4-ounce jars, leaving ¼ inch of headspace between the top of the jam and the lid. Use a bubble tool, or other nonmetallic implement, to release any trapped air. Wipe the rims, cover the jars, and screw the bands on just fingertip-tight. Process for 10 minutes. Cool for 24 hours. Check the seals and store in a cool, dark place for up to 1 year.

green bean in every way except color, and you can use them interchangeably. Using a combination of the two makes for a particularly attractive presentation in a cold-pack pickle, such as dilly beans.

Q I came back from the U-pick with buckets full! How can I process all of these berries before they fade?

A Good news! You can freeze those berries and turn them into jam as you are able. Just use the tips for freezing berries (page 142). When you have time to can, you can pull out the amount you need, transfer it straight to the jam pot — no need to defrost — and whip up your favorite recipe.

Q How can I find ripe pears?

A Pears are one fruit that can ripen off the tree. It's fine to buy them firm and then let them soften up a bit by placing them on the counter for a few days. Keep in mind that pears ripen from the inside out, so a pear that feels firm may be quite ready. The best way to check is to pinch the neck. If that top part of the pear, by the stem end, is beginning to soften, your pear is ready to go. Be careful not to let your pears become overripe, as soft pears can have a gritty texture and won't perform well in your recipes.

Q What's the difference between hard-neck and soft-neck garlic?

A If you buy your garlic in the grocery store, chances are you are eating soft-neck garlic. This is the most popular variety available commercially. It has smaller cloves and is well covered with papery white skin.

Hard-neck garlic is often available in farmers' markets. It doesn't keep as well, due in part to having only a thin,

hard-neck garlic

soft-neck garlic

garlic scapes

white, papery covering. But it does offer a bonus crop — it sprouts the garlic scapes that are trimmed back in the spring to encourage bulb growth (and that make mighty fine eating — fresh or pickled).

Q Is there a variety of corn that is best for preserving?

A You can use any variety of corn you like in your preserving recipes. I grew up with the super-flavorful but increasingly rare Silver Queen variety and still love the taste of white-kernel corn. But you can use either white or yellow interchangeably.

Be aware that genetically modified sweet corn is quickly gaining market share, so if you are looking to avoid GMO products in your diet, make sure your cobs are labeled GMO-free or are certified organic — the only two tags that ensure the food is not genetically modified.

Keep in mind that corn is a very starchy vegetable. It must be accompanied by a heavy dose of acid to be safe for canning using the boiling water method. You can safely can un-acidified corn in a pressure canner. It also freezes and dries well.

Prolonging Produce

Q I've heard that some produce keeps better out of the refrigerator.

A It's true. Some produce will rapidly lose flavor and texture if it is chilled. The cold temperatures quickly convert the sugars to starch, leaving the produce tasting bland rather than sweet.

- **Tomatoes.** Never refrigerate; store stem-side down at room temperature.

- **Onions.** Store in a cool, dark place, but never next to potatoes, as these relatives of the lily family emit gas that will accelerate the potatoes' decay.

- **Potatoes.** Store in a cool, dark place. Exposure to light develops a compound called solanine, which results in an emerald green tinge to the tuber. In excessive quantities, solanine can be toxic, so be sure to discard very green potatoes.

- **Basil.** Never refrigerate or it will turn black almost instantly. Set the cut stems in a glass of water, like a bouquet of flowers, and leave on your counter.

- **Melons.** They go mealy under extended refrigeration. If you like your melon chilled, you can pop it in the icebox for a few hours to lower its temperature. But its texture will be best if it is left at room temperature for the most part and chilled only briefly just before eating. You can refrigerate any uneaten portion of your melon, but the sooner it makes its way to your plate, the better off you will be. If you don't get to the melon for a few days, you might enjoy it juiced so that texture is no longer an issue.

Q Why is it important to store some produce in damp sand?

A Maintaining the proper moisture levels for your root cellar produce is critical to effective storage. Keeping food in an environment that is too dry is just as detrimental as one that is too moist. Damp sand provides the perfect balance for some foods, such as carrots and beets, that would quickly wither without a good dose of humidity. To store produce in damp sand:

1. Mix your sand in a large container with water until it feels moist to the touch but not wet.

2. Fill a bucket or other container with 2 inches of the dampened sand.

3. Add a layer of produce and cover by 2 inches with the dampened sand.

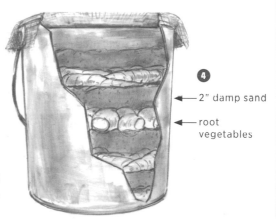

4. Continue layering until you are about 2 inches below the top of your bucket.

2" damp sand

root vegetables

5. Cover with a wire-mesh screen to prevent pests from accessing your stash.

6. Spray occasionally with water to keep the sand damp.

Q Which kind of cabbage is best for long-term storage?

A Fresh, compact heads of cabbage are best for storage. Red and green store equally well and can be used interchangeably in recipes. Open-headed cabbages such as Napa wilt too quickly to be considered for long-term storage.

To store compact heads of cabbage, wrap them individually in newspaper and place on shelves in a cool cellar or your refrigerator. Spritz occasionally with water to keep the leaves from drying out. Kept in this way, they will stay fresh for 1 to 3 months. Remove any withered leaves before using.

Q What is the best way to store apples?

A No one likes a mealy apple. Leave them out at room temperature and they will turn to sawdust in a heartbeat. To keep your pommes fresh and crunchy, keep them cool. A root cellar is good, or you can put them in your fridge if you don't have a cellar rigged up. Wherever you put them, keep in mind that they give off a lot of ethylene gas that will ripen to the point of rot any produce in their midst. So store apples separate from other fruits. Even better, layer them in dry leaves in a bucket in your cellar or wrap them individually in newspaper to help them keep their gas to themselves.

Some apples are better for storage than others. These so-called keepers maintain their texture and flavor well into the fall and sometimes longer. Ask your farmer for the keepers that they offer or look for these varieties:

- Arkansas Black
- Baldwin
- Cortland
- Empire
- Enterprise
- Fuji
- Jonagold
- Northern Spy
- Roxbury Russet
- Suncrisp

Q How can I keep asparagus fresh?

A Some foods, such as asparagus, require extra attention to retain their flavor. For best results, trim bottoms and stand in a pan filled with a few inches of water to keep these thirsty spears hydrated. Loosely shroud with a damp paper towel and store in the fridge for no more than a few days.

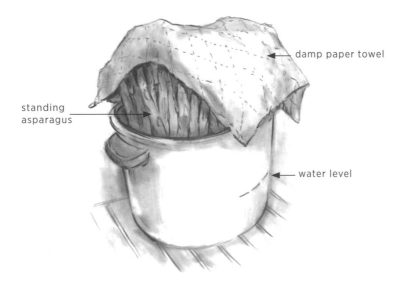

damp paper towel

standing asparagus

water level

Q Why don't my local berries last as long as those I buy in the store?

A It may sound counterintuitive, but farm-fresh food will often tire on the counter sooner than store-bought produce. Several factors contribute to this:

- Farm-fresh food is allowed to ripen on the vine and is sold at its peak of freshness. Store-bought produce is picked unripe so it can survive the travel — a minimum of 6 days from a field in California to a produce department on the East Coast — storage, and display time. So essentially, the produce in the store has yet to ripen, which is why it stays firm for a longer period of time.

- Produce on display in the grocery store is often sprayed with fungicides and waxes to make it last longer on the shelf.

- The varieties of produce available in the grocery store are often selected for durability, not flavor. They may last longer, but they won't taste better.

Q What is the best way to store berries?

A Berries hold up best in a not-too-cold part of the refrigerator. I never rinse until I am ready to use them. Some eaters have reported to me that they give their sturdier berries a little swish in some water laced with white vinegar and this prolongs their shelf life in the fridge; the ratio is one part vinegar to ten parts water. You can re-rinse before using if you detect a whiff of vinegar on the fruit.

CHAPTER 3

Prep Work

You don't have to be a master chef to preserve your own food. But it will help to have a basic understanding of different ways to ready your raw produce for the process. Here are some basic terms and techniques you can use to make your work easier and more efficient.

Kitchen Skills

Q I am very careful about cross-contaminating surfaces when I cook with meat, but I hear you can get sick from contaminated produce, too. What's a cook to do?

A It's true. Produce can carry some of the same contaminating pathogens that lead to food-borne illness in meat. To protect yourself, always wash produce carefully before it gets to the cutting board. You don't need any special sprays or washes; just lots of cold running water will do in most cases. If I am washing fruits and vegetables with rinds or skins that are very dirty or porous, such as cantaloupe, I give them an extra scrub with unscented dish soap and a sturdy vegetable brush and rinse thoroughly. Even foods that you are going to peel need to be thoroughly washed before removing their outer layer to avoid creating a contaminating soup when the juice from the cut fruit mixes with any dirt left on the peels.

Q Can I chop my ingredients in the food processor?

A A food processor can chew through a lot of produce quickly, but it can't always give you the texture you need for a good result. Some recipes will indicate when the machine is appropriate. I find it helpful when I want to shred ingredients, such as horseradish root, or when I need to slice items such as citrus peels for marmalades. It does a good puree. However, I don't find the mechanized wonder very good at chopping or dicing ingredients.

When you are staring down pounds of produce that need to be diced for a recipe, such as relish or salsa, it can be very tempting to run them through the food processor rather than chop them by hand. What you gain in efficiency, however, you may lose in quality. The pieces are often uneven — some are very finely minced, while others are in larger chunks — so they won't cook at the same rate. This will compromise the texture of your finished product.

If you find that the dicing is too tedious, I would suggest either finding another recipe to use up your produce — you can slice cukes into chips for pickles more quickly than dicing them for relish — or enlisting a friend to help with the chore. Many hands make fast — and fun — work out of such projects.

Q Do I need a fancy knife?

A You do not need a fancy knife, but you do need a sharp one. A nice, heavy knife that feels good in your hand will make your prep work less tedious and will help you avoid the muscle strain that often comes with a repetitive physical task.

You don't need a wide assortment of knives. A sturdy chef's knife, with at least a 6-inch blade, is good for most chopping and dicing. A paring knife is helpful for small work, such as peeling.

Sharpen your knives frequently. Dull knives crush food rather than slice it. Dull knives also slip more often, making them more dangerous to use.

Kitchen Tip

Want to know if your knife has a good edge? Hold it, cutting edge toward you, and tilt it back and forth. A dull blade will reflect a thin strip of light back at you — almost like the knife has a hair-thin mirror on its edge, reflecting a beam of sunlight in your eye. A sharp blade will reflect no light at all.

Q How do I sharpen a knife?

A If you could see the edge of your knife under a microscope, you would notice that it isn't really an edge at all, but more like a row of well-aligned teeth. When the knife is sharp, the teeth slice through the food in a clean line. When the knife is dull, the teeth are out of alignment and the knife gnaws raggedly through the food, tearing it roughly and often slipping rather than slicing. A good knife with a finely honed edge is the key to much kitchen success.

Keeping Your Knives Sharp

Always wash your knives by hand. The high temperatures, caustic chemicals, and jostling of the dishwasher will rapidly deteriorate the edge of the blade.

Keep your knives clean. By this, I don't mean wash them frequently, but wipe them off immediately after cutting. This is particularly true when you are working with acidic foods, such as lemons. The acids in such foods immediately begin to act on the metal and will dull your blade quickly if not removed.

Visit a professional knife sharpener occasionally. A pro will re-hone the edge of a well-used blade. This will give your knife a new life and save you frustration, and maybe even some nicks and cuts, in the kitchen.

Use a steel to realign the teeth of your blade. This is helpful between visits to the knife sharpener. Hold the knife at a 20-degree angle to the steel and swipe downward, as if you are cutting off a thin slice of beef from a roast. Be sure to pull the entire knife blade across the steel, from hilt to tip, for even sharpening.

Use a stone to sharpen your knives. Often you will find a sharpening stone with two different grains on either side, coarse and fine, or even triangular stones with three grains: coarse, medium, and fine. Some stones are meant to be lubricated with water, others with oil. Check the instructions that come with your stone to determine the best lubricant. Begin honing on the coarsest grain of stone. Angle your knife at a 20-degree pitch away from the stone and gently rub it away from the blade edge, in smooth circles. Flip over the knife and repeat on the other side. Progress to the finer grains on your stone, continuing to rub it away from the blade in small circles. Wipe your blade well before using.

Q What's the difference between chopping, dicing, and mincing?

A It's important to prep your food as your recipe indicates, so these are good terms to know. Cut your produce too large and it won't process thoroughly. Cut it too finely and it may turn to mush. *Chopping*, *dicing*, and *mincing* are terms used to describe the size of the cut.

Chopping connotes large pieces of produce, usually of imprecise measurement unless indicated. Chopping increases surface area so that food cooks more quickly and is used when texture isn't important. Apples are often described as being "chopped" in preparation for sauce making.

Dicing is cutting food into small squares; the size can vary and is often indicated in the recipe. The size of the cube is usually ¼ inch to ½ inch. Produce for salsas, relishes, and chutneys is often diced.

Mincing means pulverizing items, such as garlic or ginger, into a fine texture, almost a paste. A quick method for mincing is to first use your knife to smash the food. Position your garlic clove or a coin of ginger on the cutting board. Turn your knife so that it is parallel to the board, and then rest the heel of the blade (the part nearest the handle) on top of the item. Quickly and forcefully strike the heel of the blade with the heel of your hand to pulverize the food. Then flip the knife, cutting-edge down, and quickly chop through the mash until you achieve the desired texture.

diced tomatoes

chopped tomatoes

minced garlic

Q What is a chiffonade?

A *Chiffonade* means to cut something into "little rags." It's a preparation usually applied to leafy vegetables, such as basil or kale. The leaves are laid flat and stacked on top of each other. They are rolled up like a cigar and finely sliced crosswise, effectively cutting them into little shreds.

Q What's the difference between a simmer and a rolling boil?

A *Simmer* and *full* (or *rolling*) *boil* describe different temperatures of heated liquids. As you apply more heat to your pot, the temperature will rise, moving your ingredients through these phases of increased agitation. The higher heat causes evaporating vapors to rise more quickly, creating a bubbling action throughout the food.

Simmering describes a gentle bubbling on the surface of the food. It occurs when the recipe reaches a temperature of 185 to 200°F at sea level (the boiling point decreases as you climb in altitude).

A *full boil* occurs when the temperature reaches 212°F at sea level. Large bubbles pop excitedly in rapid succession on the surface of the liquid.

You may come across in-between directives such as *strong simmer* and *gentle boil* that describe a range of increased activity in the pot.

Q What does it mean to reduce something?

A *Reduce* means to cook something down in volume. Reducing concentrates flavors and often thickens liquids and sauces.

Pan reductions are sauces that are made by adding liquid to a pan in which food has been sautéed and then cooking the sauce down (reducing it) until it has a stronger flavor and a slightly more viscous quality.

Blanching

Q Why is it important to blanch food?

A Blanching food serves a number of purposes:

- As counterintuitive as it is, this wet process is often necessary for food to dry properly. The boiling softens and splits skins, allowing moisture to evaporate more readily and completely.

- It is useful in removing skins from fruits such as peaches and tomatoes. The heat causes the skin to loosen from the fruit so that it slips away from the flesh easily.

- It sets the colors of foods so that they stay bright in storage. The brief dip in boiling water releases some of the air trapped in the cell walls of the produce, making the colors appear more intense.

- Blanching coaxes liquid out of produce so that it forms fewer ice crystals during freezing.

- Most important, blanching helps to deactivate enzymes that can hasten deterioration. This is particularly important for frozen food, as low temperatures will slow decay but not halt it completely. By blanching food, you give it its longest possible life in the freezer.

Q When I'm blanching produce, do I have to plunge it into ice water or can I just let it cool at room temperature?

A The ice bath is an important step in blanching produce. It stops the cooking quickly so that only the outside of the fruit is exposed to heat, while the inside remains raw. If you skip this step, you run the risk of cooking your fruit all the way through. It will become soft and hard to handle and will give you less-than-desirable results in your final recipe.

Kitchen Tip

If you have extra freezer space, keep a bag of ice on hand for blanching. It will be one less thing to remember and lug home on preserving day.

Blanching, Step by Step

Blanching is easy. Here's how to do it:

1. Have ready a large bowl of ice water; about 4 cups of ice to every 1 gallon of water will chill it nicely.

2. Bring a large pot of water, at least 1 gallon, to a boil.

3. Drop your produce, no more than 1 pound at a time, into the boiling water. (If you overload your pot, it will take a long time for it to return to temperature, and your food will likely over-cook while you're waiting for the water to return to a boil.)

4. After about 30 seconds, check your produce. Fruits will split and vegetables will brighten in color when they are ready. This should take no more than a minute.

5. Scoop your produce out of the pot with a slotted spoon or wire spider and plunge it into the ice water to shock it and stop the residual heat from cooking it through.

Blanch: Submerge produce in boiling water for 30 to 60 seconds.

6. Once it has cooled completely, scoop your produce out of the ice bath and dry it thoroughly on paper or tea towels.

Note: Small items, such as peas, can be tedious to separate from the ice after shocking. Rather than dumping them loose into the ice bath, you can scoop them out of

Shock: Transfer to ice water to cool completely.

the boiling water with a large strainer and lower the strainer filled with peas into the ice bath, swirling it occasionally to circulate iced water around the cooling produce.

Peels and Pits

Q What's the best way to peel and core apples?

A There are a few different ways to peel and core apples. However you do it, be sure to submerge your apples, as you go, in an acidic solution (¼ cup lemon juice mixed with 2 cups water) to prevent browning.

apple corer

The low-tech version is just to use a paring knife to whittle off the skin, slice the fruit in half, and carve out the core.

You can also use an apple corer, which is an instrument with a handle attached to a hollow metal tube with serrated edges on one end; plunge it through the apple from stem to blossom end to excavate the core.

And if you find yourself with a lot of apples, or if you just like fun gadgets, you can invest in an apple peeler/corer machine. This is a hand-cranked apparatus that simultaneously bores the core out while slicing the peel off in ribbons as you use the handle to spin the fruit around the cutting edges of the machine. Some machines offer the added functionality of simultaneously slicing the apple as it peels the fruit.

Using an apple peeler/corer

If you are making applesauce, there is no need to peel and core at all. Just pluck off the stems, coarsely chop the fruit, cook it until soft, and run it through a food mill.

Q What's the difference between clingstone and freestone peaches?

A Stone fruits, such as peaches and plums, come in two broad categories: clingstone and freestone. Generally, the clingstone fruits come earlier in the season and freestone varieties ripen later. Which one you use depends on your recipe.

Clingstone. The flesh of clingstone fruit adheres, or clings, to the pit. It has to be cut away from the stone to be used in recipes. Because you have to whittle away the flesh from the stone, these fruits are best used in recipes where they will be cut or diced, such as in salsas and sauces.

Prepping Peaches

Slipping off the skins

Freestone. The pits of freestone fruits pop out easily when the fruit is sliced in half. Because the flesh of these fruits remains intact, you can use freestone fruit in recipes where you want to show off big slices or halved fruits. Of course, you can chop and dice the halves into salsas and sauces as well.

Removing the core from freestone fruit

Q What part of the fruit is the zest?

A Recipes often call for zest from citrus fruits. The zest is the outermost layer of the fruit's skin. Although it is very thin, it is full of the citrus oil that carries so much of the flavor of the fruit. There are several methods for removing the zest from fruits. However you remove the zest, be careful not to take the very bitter white pith that lies just beneath it. Shave off only the very top, colorful layer of peel for intense fruit flavor.

Zester. You can use a specially designed zester to remove thin ribbons of zest. This tool looks like a tiny paddle with a row of holes along its edge. Zesters are commonly part of a bartending tool set.

Removing zest with a zester

Grater. You can grate the zest from the fruit using a Microplane or the flat slits on a box grater. Just run the fruit across the teeth of the grater, turning the fruit with each swipe so that you don't grate down into the pith.

Peeler. The easiest way to remove zest is with a vegetable peeler, which cuts it off in wide ribbons. You can then julienne or mince the zest to suit your recipe.

Q Should I peel my peppers before using them in recipes?

A You don't need to peel peppers when using them in recipes — I imagine the process would be quite tedious. When canned whole or in slices, the skins help the peppers maintain their shape. Cooking diced or chopped peppers tenderizes the skin so it isn't really noticeable in such recipes as salsa and relish.

The only time you can and should peel your peppers is when you roast them. In that process (page 218), the skins are completely blackened and then they slip right off.

Q Why is it so important to remove the blossom ends from produce?

A The blossom ends of produce items (the end without a stem) such as cucumbers contain a high level of enzymes that can act on the rest of the produce in the recipe, turning it mushy. Eaters who complain of soft pickles often have failed to cut off the ends of their cucumbers. The ends often have a little bit of a bitter taste as well. For best results, carefully slice off about ¼ inch of the blossom end of your produce before preserving.

Q How do you remove the corn kernels from the cob?

A With company, if you can! Stripping corn from its cob can take some time, so it's helpful to grab a buddy or just enjoy the Zen of it. Here are some tips:

- If you are going to process a large quantity of corn, I suggest that you take the party outside, as it can be a pretty messy process. Set a picnic or folding table in a shady spot and cover it with a washable tablecloth for easy cleanup.

- If you are working indoors, you might prefer to work in a very large bowl to catch as many of the flying kernels as you can.

- I find it useful to break shucked cobs in half; the broken ends give you rather flat ends that are easier to balance. Place your cob half, cut-side down, on a cutting board, holding the cob upright by its tip.

- There are a number of tools on the market to help with the task, but I find a nice sharp chef's knife gets the job done pretty quickly. Carefully cut the kernels away from the cob by placing your knife below your fingers at about a 20-degree downward angle. Be careful not to angle in too sharply toward the cob or you will get pieces of it in with the kernels. Work your way around the cob until all of the kernels are free.

And remember, corncobs make sweet, delicious stock. Boil up a pot of them for 30 to 40 minutes and freeze the sweet liquid to flavor soups and risottos.

Q What's the best way to skin beets for pickling?

A Skinning beets is simple, though somewhat messy, prep. You need to cook them before you pickle them, so that's the first step. Cooking the beets also makes removing the skins a lot easier. Prepare your beets in one of these ways and they're ready for the pickle pot:

- **Boiling:** Trim the ends, submerge the beets in cold water, bring to a boil, and simmer until they are nearly tender, 20 to 30 minutes. Drain and cool to the touch, then proceed to peel as described below.

- **Roasting:** Wash the beets, wrap them individually in foil, and place on a cookie sheet in a 375°F oven until nearly tender, about 1 hour. Unwrap, let cool to room temperature, and peel as described below.

- **Peeling:** The peels of both boiled and roasted beets should slip off easily. (If you are not a fan of pink hands, you might want to wear gloves for this part, as the beets will stain your hands a shockingly bright fuchsia color.) You can use a paring knife to whittle away any tough spots. Now they are ready to slice or dice, as your recipe indicates.

Q I've never preserved rhubarb before. How do I prepare the stalks?

A Rhubarb isn't a very popular item in the United States, but it seems to be gaining a bit of ground as the local food movement blossoms. This is great news, as rhubarb grows prolifically once planted, giving an abundant amount of fruit with little fuss. After it is established, rhubarb grows like a weed, so it's easy to add to your garden plan. Rhubarb has a bright, citrusy flavor — so welcome when it comes to the market in the spring, particularly in areas that don't grow citrus.

But you have to be careful of one thing — the leaves. **The leaves of rhubarb are poisonous!** They must be completely trimmed from the ribs and must never be given to animals or put in the compost.

The stalks, which are the edible part of the plant, can vary in color from red to pink to green. Color does not indicate ripeness. They are all equally flavorful. But the color will transfer to your recipe. So, if you are looking for pretty pink jam, it's best to stick with the rosy stalks and leave the green ones for crumbles and pies, where the color of green stalks can be masked by a crust.

Once the stalks are trimmed of leaves, cut off any dried ends, as you would with celery, and chop or dice, as indicated in your recipe.

Q Do I have to peel carrots before pickling them?

A I don't always peel my carrots. If they are young and sweet, you can just give them a good scrub. Red carrots, such as Atomic Reds, have a gorgeous red skin that seems a shame to peel off. You can leave that on, too, but know that the carrots will not retain their gorgeous color during cooking, giving it up to the brine and other vegetables in the jar.

The skin on older carrots can be tough and somewhat bitter. It's best to peel that away. If you have the time, it's nice to *turn* the frond end of the carrot by carefully paring most of it away while still retaining a bit of its green color. It might seem tedious, but that little hint of green looks so great in the jar and separates the hand-grown carrot from the commercial ones that are so uniformly orange (and bland).

RASPBERRY JELLY

Makes about 3 cups

This jelly has all of the tangy taste of the berries without the bother of the pips. It comes out gorgeously clear and sparkling and full of that rich, red berry flavor. Be sure not to press on the fruit as it drains, as this will cloud your jelly; it will still taste great but it will lack the gemlike shimmer of a patiently made jelly.

INGREDIENTS

2 quarts raspberries (about 3 pounds)

1/4 cup water

2 cups sugar

3 teaspoons Pomona's Universal Pectin

1/4 cup bottled lemon juice

3 teaspoons calcium water
(from the Pomona's Universal Pectin kit)

PREPARE

1. Combine the berries and water in a medium nonreactive saucepan and slowly bring to a simmer. Reduce the heat to low and gently simmer for 5 minutes to release the fruit's juices, being careful not to crush or press the fruit, which will cloud your jelly.

2. Line a colander with a triple layer of cheesecloth or have ready a jelly bag in its frame, and set either device over a bowl. Remove the fruit from the heat and gently pour into your straining setup. Allow the cooked fruit to drain until all the juice has been released, at least 2 hours. Do not press on the draining fruit.

3. Combine the sugar and pectin in a small bowl.

4. Measure 2 cups of the strained juice into a medium nonreactive saucepan. Bring to a boil and stir in the lemon juice and calcium water. Sprinkle in the pectin mixture, stirring constantly to combine thoroughly. Return to a boil and simmer for 1 to 2 minutes, stirring constantly to dissolve the mixture.

5. Remove from the heat. Allow the jam to rest for 5 minutes, giving it an occasional gentle stir to release trapped air; it will thicken slightly. Skim off any foam.

PRESERVE

Refrigerate: Ladle into bowls or jars. Cool, cover, and refrigerate for up to 3 weeks.

Can. Use the boiling-water method (see page 95). Ladle the jam into clean, hot 4-ounce or half-pint jars, leaving ¼ inch of headspace between the top of the jelly and the lid. Use a bubble tool, or other nonmetallic implement, to release any trapped air. Wipe the rims, cover the jars, and screw the bands on just fingertip-tight. Process for 10 minutes. Cool for 24 hours. Check the seals and store in a cool, dark place for up to 1 year.

Raspberry flavor without the pips

Some people love the crunchy seeds from raspberries and blackberries, while others choose to avoid them. I am somewhere in between: a few pips are fine but I don't want to feel like I am chewing through gravel to get to my toast.

Often berries that contain pips are used in jellies, where the process of extracting the juice leaves all of the "cavity catchers" behind. If you want to make a jam that contains no or only some pips, you can run some or all of the berries through a fine-mesh food mill.

Q How do you pit cherries?

A As much as I try to keep my gadgets to a minimum, it really helps to have a cherry pitter when it comes time to remove the stones from the fruit. The kind I have is sort of like a pair of pliers, but rather than pincers on the end, it has an empty-bottomed cup on one side and a little prong on the other side of the calipers. You place a cherry in the cup and squeeze the pitter closed, which forces the prong through the fruit and pops out the pit in one motion. I keep several pitters in my drawer and enlist helping hands during the cherry season — it makes for fast work. If you don't have a pitter, here are two other pitting methods:

- Lay individual cherries on a cutting board and press them with the flat side of a chef's knife, as you would do with olives. The cherry will split and you can pinch out the pit. This method isn't as tidy as the pitter, but it will get the job done in a pinch.

- If you are looking to delicately extract the pits from the cherries, try this trick with a paper clip. Open up the paper clip so that you have two hooked ends. Gently insert one of the ends into the base of the cherry and use it to scoop out the pit without piercing through to the other side: tedious but effective.

Q Many recipes call for seeding cucumbers and zucchini. How do you do that?

A Many eaters who believe they cannot digest cucumbers are really reacting to the seeds. Removing them can make your cukes "burpless." The seeds can also be bitter when overdeveloped, so removing them can give you a sweeter result.

Seeding cucumbers, zucchini, and squash is easy. Just cut the vegetable in half lengthwise, and use a spoon to scoop out the seeds from its center.

Q How do you prepare plum tomatoes for canning?

A Prepping tomatoes requires a bit of work. But come the dead of winter, you will be so glad you took the extra time to have this delicious product on hand all year long. Here's how you do it.

1. Have ready a large bowl, impeccably clean sink, or cooler filled with an ice bath (about 4 cups of ice to every 1 gallon of cold water).

2. Bring a large pot of water to a boil.

3. Blanch the tomatoes by dropping them into the hot water in batches, no more than six at a time. (See Blanching, page 39.)

4. When they start to split, after 30 to 60 seconds, scoop them out and shock them by plunging them into the ice bath. This will loosen the skin and keep them from cooking through.

5. Repeat with the remaining tomatoes. Drain.

6. Using an apple corer, remove the core and seeds by plunging the utensil through the fruit from stem to blossom end. Discard core. Repeat with remaining tomatoes.

7. Using a paring knife to grasp the skin of the tomato, pull the skin away from the flesh. It should slip off easily. Any small bits of skin can be pared away with the knife. If the skin is clinging stubbornly to the fruit, dip the tomato back into the hot water, then shock it in the ice bath and try again.

8. Repeat with remaining tomatoes. Tomatoes are now recipe-ready.

You can enlist a group of friends to help with the work. Set them up assembly-line style, with one person blanching and shocking, another coring, and one peeling. You'll have a year's supply of tomatoes put up in no time.

Kitchen Tip

Collect the tomato juice released in the prepping process: do your coring and peeling over a bowl lined with cheesecloth or a fine-mesh sieve. You can toss your trimmings in there as you work. When your tomatoes are all prepped, squeeze the cores and skins through the sieve to extract as much juice as possible and you'll have a lively, refreshing beverage as payment for your troubles.

Making the Most of It

Q I love making pickled beets but hate throwing away all those greens. Is there anything I can do with them?

A Beet greens, and those from turnips as well, taste great sautéed. When you are pickling these vegetables and find yourself with a tangle of them, give them a good wash, spin them dry, roughly chop, and sauté in olive oil and garlic. Cooked this way, you can enjoy them as a side, toss them with pasta or white beans, add them to some broth, or top them with a poached egg for a twist on eggs Florentine.

Too many to enjoy at one sitting? The sautéed greens keep, refrigerated, for 3 to 5 days, or you can transfer them to an airtight container and freeze. Thaw before using or add directly to soups and stews.

Q I see fennel in my market, but I'm not sure which part you eat.

A Fennel is a terrific vegetable to work into your repertoire. It has a light licorice flavor that is bright and refreshing when served raw and takes on a more mellow sweetness when cooked.

You can think of the fennel as having three parts: the fronds at the top and the bulb at the bottom, both connected by the stem. The fronds can be used as you would dill, chopped and added as a fresh herb to dishes; it's a terrific garnish for fish. The stem can be tough but has good flavor. Chop it and add it to stocks and soups — like the rest of the plant, it has a licorice flavor.

When a recipe calls for fennel as a produce ingredient, this most likely refers to the bulb part of the plant. Here's how to prep it. Cut it away from the stem. Trim off the bottom, root end. Slice the bulb in half vertically to reveal the tough core inside the bulb. Pare out the core. You can shave, dice, or chop the bulb as your recipe indicates. Try it shaved in salads

Fennel

bulb   stem   sliced

fronds

with citrus and Parmesan, cut into chunks and roasted with an equal amount of carrots, or diced and added to fish stew.

Q Can I eat cauliflower leaves?

A The first time I saw a cauliflower in the farmers' market, I thought it was just the prettiest thing — a flower indeed. With creamy florets swaddled in gorgeous leaves, it really is so different from the prewrapped shrunken heads you see on supermarket shelves. And now, with heirloom varieties becoming increasingly available, there are all kinds of beautiful cauliflowers from which to choose. And, good news: You can eat the leaves, too. Sauté them in garlic and olive oil just as you would a leafy green, or purée them with garlic, a bit of Parmesan, and some nuts for a quick pesto. Waste not, want not (particularly when it is fresh and local)!

Q All of these peels add up to a lot of material. Is there anything I can do with it?

A When you are canning, the pile of peels, seeds, and cores can mount up quickly. Some of the ends can be used in companion recipes. Apple peels can be turned into pectin (page 194). Beet and turnip greens can be sautéed. Onion skins, carrot trimmings, mushroom stems, and garlic peels can be used to make stocks.

On the other hand, some kitchen scrap is just that: scrap material. Draining juice for jelly can leave you with a fair amount of fruit pulp. While some swear by adding these bits to their smoothies, I find that the seeds can have a bitter taste.

The best way to get some use out of produce scraps that aren't edible is to turn them into rich, life-giving compost. There are a variety of containers on the market that allow you to compost on a small scale. If a worm bucket in your kitchen doesn't appeal, there are barrel-size containers for use outdoors. They have handles that allow you to turn them regularly and easily.

Whichever method you choose, be sure to layer your kitchen scraps with brown yard scraps, such as dry leaves, to keep the compost active and sweet. Don't make the mistake I did and start piling all of your yard rubbish on top, or you will just create a heap, not a compost pile.

Well-rotted compost is a great addition to the garden. Use it to "feed" your next crop and you'll keep the circle going.

Q **Can I use cherry and peach pits in my recipes?**

A The pits of stone fruits such as peaches, apricots, plums, and cherries contain a small amount of cyanide. While swallowing the occasional cherry pit won't hurt you, it's not a good idea to use a lot of them in your cooking. Some older recipes call for peach kernels to be added to the cooking fruit to impart a subtle almond flavor. And you still may see stone fruit kernels for sale; these are specially processed to remove the cyanide. Call me a nervous Nelly, but I am not a big fan of any recipe that comes with a recommended dosage disclaimer. Rather than adding the pits to your recipe, you can stir in a small amount, ¼ to ½ teaspoon, of almond extract to get a similar nutty flavor without worrying about the cyanide exposure.

Kitchen Tips

Q **Can I use waxed paper instead of parchment?**

A Waxed paper and parchment paper look very similar. They are both translucent, coated papers. But they have very different uses and are not interchangeable.

Waxed paper is, as its name indicates, paper that has been coated with wax. It's great for wrapping sandwiches and keeping cheese fresh in the fridge. It makes a terrific layer between the jar and lid of vinegar infusions to keep the acid from reacting with the metal top. However, the wax will melt if heated, so waxed paper is not an option as a baking sheet liner that is headed for the oven.

Parchment paper, on the other hand, is coated with silicone. It is heat-resistant so you can use it in the oven (though it will darken at very high temperatures and burn under the broiler). Parchment paper is often used to line baking sheets and pans because its non-stick coating helps even the stickiest foods release easily.

Q My recipe calls for an immersion blender but I don't have one. Is there something else I can use?

A I find an immersion blender very helpful and a good investment, so I frequently use it in recipes. I am not big on gadgets, however, so I can relate to the pared-down kitchen and can offer some alternatives.

- The most low-tech solution would be to use a food mill. It is an essential tool for making applesauce and is great for seeding and peeling tomatoes for sauce as well. If you are someone who does a fair amount of home food preservation, you will get a lot of use out of it.

- You can also use a standard upright blender. Carefully ladle the ingredients you wish to purée into the blender, being careful not to fill it beyond three-quarters of its total capacity. Cover the top with a tea towel and press down on the lid during processing to ensure that it doesn't come off and spray you with hot ingredients while you are blending. Work in small batches until your entire batch of ingredients has been puréed.

- Alternatively, you can use a food processor fitted with a chopping blade to purée your recipe. Treat it like the blender, being careful not to overfill, and cover it with a tea towel during processing to avoid a hot mess.

Q What is a food mill?

A A food mill is a hand-cranked food grinder. It's used to purée cooked foods such as apples while simultaneously removing their seeds and skins. Food mills often come with screens in a variety of densities for creating fine or coarse purées.

To use a food mill:

1. Place the mill over a heatproof bowl or pot.

2. Fill it halfway with cooked food and turn the handle clockwise to press it through the puréeing screen.

3. Every third turn or so, reverse direction for a turn or two to release trapped seeds and skins, and then resume turning the crank in a clockwise direction.

4. Repeat with remaining cooked produce, emptying the mill of skins and pits as necessary.

Q **What's the best way to measure produce for preserving?**

A It's important to be careful about the measurements in your recipe and to follow them accurately to achieve consistent, reliable results. Weight is the most accurate measurement for foods you are planning to preserve. Volume can vary. For example, 1 quart of large berries can have a lot less plant material than 1 quart of small berries that might fit into your cup more compactly. A kitchen scale is convenient to have on hand, but if you don't have one, you can ask your produce to be weighed at the point of purchase. Be sure to mark the weight on your bag so you don't forget it by the time you get to the kitchen.

For ingredients such as a clove of garlic or a medium onion, there is no need to measure; just be sure that you follow the description given.

Q **There are so many different salts on the market. Does it matter which one I use in my recipe?**

A The kind of salt you use in your recipe can affect the end result. Salts come with their own characteristic flavors. The size of their crystals will also determine how densely they measure — 1 cup of one kind of salt may be much lighter (and bring much less salty flavor to your recipe) than 1 cup of another. You don't need to buy specialized salts, but you should know how the varying salts differ and how they will impact your recipe.

Kitchen Tip

Spices can lose their flavor and even take on a musty taste and smell as they age. Keep your spices fresh by storing them in a cool, dark place and rotating them out regularly. Make sure they pass the sniff test before using — give the jar a whiff; if it doesn't smell good, it won't taste good. Freshly ground spices will always have more flavor than preground. Giving them a whir in a clean coffee grinder will do the trick.

A Glossary of Salt

Mineralized sea salt. Many finishing salts, as they are often called, are sea salts that bring a distinct texture and sometimes an intense flavor to the dish. The minerals in these sea salts can color your produce and color and cloud brines. Some highly flavored salts, such as Indian black salt, which smells strongly of sulfur, can overwhelm your recipe.

Sea salt. Many canners choose to use white, pourable sea salt in their recipes because they claim the trace minerals help to firm the texture of their produce.

Table salt. This salt often contains additives such as anti-caking agents and iodine, which are flavorless but can cloud your brine and color your produce in the jar. Its angular crystal shape makes it difficult to dissolve in cold brines. Table salt is quite dense, measuring 1⅓ cups per pound.

Canning salt. This specially produced salt made for home food preservation has a very flaky texture, so it dissolves quickly in recipes. It contains no additives that will interfere with the color, texture, or flavor of your recipe. Canning salt measures 1⅓ cups per pound.

Kosher salt. Fast becoming the salt of choice in both home and professional kitchens, kosher salt is inexpensive and readily available and is my preferred salt for home food preservation. It is produced without the anti-caking agents and mineral additives found in table salt. The flaky shape of the crystals in kosher salt ensures that it dissolves more easily than table salt. Kosher salts can have varying crystal sizes, which will affect the amount of salt contained in equal measures, so adjust your recipe accordingly to get a consistent flavor. Morton brand kosher salt measures 1½ cups for every pound of salt, while Diamond brand measures 1⅔ cups for every pound.

PART 2

Preserving Processes

*H*ome food preservation — it's not just about canning. Drying, infusing, fermenting, even stashing food in your fridge or freezer, are all terrific ways to preserve the flavors of the season. In this section, you'll find answers to the most frequently asked questions about all of these processes.

Consider Preserving Processes your technique cheat sheet. This part of the book covers the hows and whys of the ways we preserve food. You'll know when you need to pressure can and when you don't and the best way to do it. You'll learn how to spot trouble so you can stay out of it. And a few recipes are thrown in so you can run some water through the pipes. After all, we're not just here for information — we're here for a good dinner!

CHAPTER 4

General Canning

There are two kinds of canning: the boiling-water method and pressure canning. While each type of canning has its own unique set of concerns, there are some issues that are common to both. Here is an overview of general canning information to start you on your way.

But first, let's just start with the number-one question:

Q **Is canning dangerous?**

A Canning is as dangerous as any other type of cooking. Careful, clean preparation and trusted processes are essential to a good outcome. But if you can boil water and follow some very basic kitchen–common sense rules, there's nothing to fear.

Here are the golden rules. Always:

- Follow your recipe.
- Use the appropriate processing time.
- Keep your work space neat and tidy.

There you have it!

Workspace

Q **Don't I need a big kitchen to can?**

A Everyone wants a giant kitchen these days, and why not? They are the center of the home, full of warmth, and a great place to hang out. For all of those reasons, a big kitchen can be a joy. But you don't need a big space to can. I have friends who manage to do just fine in the tiniest of city kitchens. Two burners and about a tea towel's worth of space is all it takes to get your can on.

The two burners will allow you to preheat your canner at the same time that you prepare your recipe for canning. You can have a cooktop larger than that, but two is the minimum number of burners you will need.

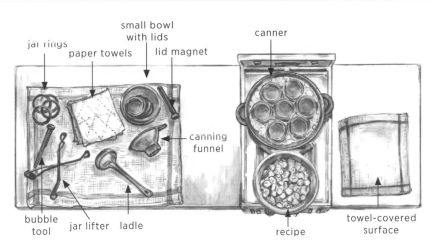

jar rings
paper towels
small bowl with lids
lid magnet
canner
canning funnel
bubble tool
jar lifter
ladle
recipe
towel-covered surface

The tea towel's worth of space is where you will lay out all of your equipment and fill and lid your jars — think of it as a filling station. Ideally it is next to your stove, but if not, you can make do. Just lay out the towel to create a filling station nearby — on the counter opposite your stove or on a nearby table or island. You can also set up a temporary space to fill and lid your jars, such as a folding table or rolling cart. It's not as convenient, but if necessary, you can even set up your filling station outside or in another room.

If the filling station is far from your stove, you might want to put down a hot pad next to it so that you have a place to set your freshly cooked jam, salsa, brine, or whatever it is you may be ladling into your jars. You may also want to set your jars on a sturdy baking sheet as you fill them so that you can easily transport the filled jars back to the heating canner. No matter where you set up your filling station or rest your filled jars, make sure it is on a stable surface — you don't want a pot of hot jam or piping-hot jars teetering on wobbly legs.

If you have another area in the kitchen, also about a tea towel big, where your jars can cool as you remove them from the canner, that's convenient. If not, line a baking sheet with another towel and use it to transport your processed jars to cool elsewhere.

Q I don't have a very fancy stove. Can I still can?

A Dedicated home cooks often talk about the power of their stoves like gearheads talk about their car's horsepower. But even a jalopy can get you down the street, and so it is with canning. All you really need are two burners of regular BTU strength (no professional cooktops needed) that are capable of boiling a large pot of water.

In fact, some pressure canners are not meant to work on high-BTU burners (check your manufacturer's instructions for BTU recommendations). While an eight-burner continuous cooktop with wok insert, griddle, and indoor grill might be nice, it won't make your jam taste any better.

Q If you could plan a canning porch, what would you put in it?

A It wasn't long ago that canning porches were common, and I say we bring them back. A little room off to the side of the house is a great place to scrub down produce and get it into jars. And what a delight to have a room outside of the day-to-day kitchen activity where the canner won't be in anyone's way and you don't have to slide everything aside to put together a little lunch.

The canning porch can be very simple. It's essentially a screened-in space so it's cooled by great air circulation but covered from rain and protected from pests. I dream of having one in my house, and when I think of it, my canning porch has these things:

- A sturdy stove top with at least two widely spaced gas burners that would allow for two big pots to sit side by side (or four burners so that I could work on two recipes simultaneously).

- At least 18 inches of counter space on both sides of the stove, with the space on the left for filling jars and the space on the right for removing them from the boiling water.

- A long counter for prep, preferably double deep so that when I am prepping with a friend, we can face each other.

- A double sink deep enough to fit a canner under the spigot on one side and a separate well for washing produce.

- Deep drawers to store bowls and colanders.

- Shallow drawers so that I can easily find equipment such as thermometers, funnels, and bubble tools.

- A deep cabinet for storing empty jars.

- A small ice maker so I always have plenty of ice on hand for blanching (a bit of a luxury item, but I did say I was dreaming).

Canning Porch

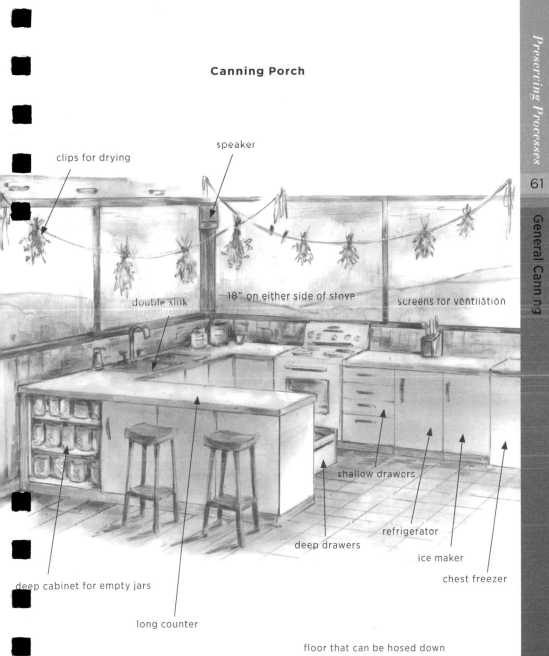

speaker

clips for drying

double sink

18" on either side of stove

screens for ventilation

shallow drawers

deep drawers

refrigerator

ice maker

chest freezer

deep cabinet for empty jars

long counter

floor that can be hosed down

- A small fridge for storing spices, lemon juice, and other perishable bits.

- A chest freezer for storing produce.

- A string of clips for quickly hanging herb bunches or chiles for drying.

- A floor that I can hose down.

- Awesome speakers and a place for the iced tea pitcher!

Q It's getting hot in here. How can we beat the heat?

A Even with a powerful AC unit going full throttle, canning can really make your kitchen cook. After all, you are bound to have at least one large cauldron of water on the boil and another pot simmering away. It can lead to some steamy moments. Here are a few ideas for beating the heat:

Can at night. I have had some of my best, most enjoyable canning sessions at night. The kids are tucked in, the house is quiet, and the air is cooler. Pop open a cold one, turn up the tunes, and get your can on.

Can outside. It's not great for pressure canning, because the heat has to be so steady to maintain pressure. But it's terrific for the boiling-water method. I have a two-burner camp stove just for the purpose. I set it out on my patio and then hose down the "kitchen" when I'm done.

Freeze your food. While not the best idea for pickles, you can freeze fruits such as berries and turn them into jam in the winter. The canning/snow day is a delight!

Give in to it. It's hot out. The canner is boiling. Add to that the effort of chopping, dicing, and stirring, and it can be a bit warm. Rather than fight the heat, give in to it. Wear your coolest clothes (or littlest clothes, you canning minx!), pull your hair back, and enjoy the sauna. (And think of how great all the humidity is for your complexion.)

Equipment

Q What kind of equipment do I need for home canning?

A As you'll see from the list that follows, there's not a lot of specialized equipment that you need to preserve your own food. The only pricey gadget on the list is the pressure canner, and you don't need that for all canning, only pressure canning.

I travel quite a bit teaching canning classes, and I load all of my equipment into a single, large suitcase. Okay, it's pretty large — we call it "the Beast." But even at that, it is a mobile canning kitchen all in one bag. It has everything I need, jars and all. It's a good idea to create your own beast if you do a lot of preserving so you can find everything easily.

At home, my beast is a rolling cart that I can pull into place in the kitchen. It has all of my preserving equipment — canner and utensils, jars, extra sugar, pectin, bottles of vinegar and lemon juice — lined up on its shelves and a place on top to put cooling jars that have just come out of the canner. It's very convenient to have everything in one place, and having the cart on wheels means that I can pull it into service whenever I like and stash it out of the way when it is not in use. If you don't have room for a cart, some big bins can hold all of your preserving needs.

If you don't have space to stash all of your canning equipment together, or if your canning equipment does double duty as your day-to-day cookware, a checklist is a good alternative. That way you can quickly gather up all of your equipment, and you won't have to go scrambling for missing bibs and bobs. Just run through the list, putting everything in its place as you go, and you will be set up in no time. Having everything in some sort of easy grab-and-go system will shave gobs of time off your preserving schedule. Without the bother of trying to remember and locate everything you'll need, you'll be that much more inclined to jump into a project.

Canning Equipment

Here are the items you need to have on hand or on your list.

Mandatory

Pressure canner (for pressure canning) and/or a boiling-water-method canner (substitute: stockpot, lobster pot, or pasta pot)

Canning jars and lids

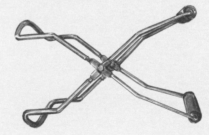

Canning tongs

Nice to have

- Kitchen scale
- Food mill or immersion blender for puréeing
- Parchment paper

- Plastic gloves for working with items such as chiles or beets
- Cherry pitter
- Peeler

Substitutable (see page 67 for details)

Canning rack (substitute: cake cooling rack, grill rack, or layer of canning jar rings [above right])

Canning funnel (substitute: small ladle or regular funnel with spout end cut off)

Bubble tool (substitute: plastic knife, chopstick, or wooden skewer)

Lid lifter (magnetic) (substitute: soft-tipped tongs or your heatproof fingers)

Smart to have

- Tea towels
- Paper towels
- Oven mitts
- Bowls of varying sizes
- Sharp knife
- Ladle
- Cutting boards
- Colander

- Whisk
- Baking sheets for carrying jars and drying food
- Measuring cups and spoons
- Indelible markers for labeling jars
- Extra lids and rings

Q Can I can on an electric stove?

A It is fine to cook on coil-top electric stoves. It may take a little longer for your canner to come to heat if the coil is much smaller than your canner, but just keep the lid on and it will get there.

Glass- or smooth-top electric stoves, however, can be tricky. The rippled bottoms of some canners do not make full contact, and the difference between the size of the canner bottom and the size of the burner can be problematic. Always check your manufacturer's instructions to see if your cooktop is canning compatible.

Q Can I can on a glass-topped stove?

A I always say that you don't have to have a super-powered stove to can, and that is true. However, glass-topped stoves can be tricky. Most canners do not have the smooth bottom that gives a pot good contact with a glass top. Additionally, canners are often larger than the diameter of the heating element, which can make it hard to get a full boil; if it does get hot, the overhang can damage the cooktop, possibly causing it to crack or shatter. Always check with the manufacturer to see if they recommend canning on your stovetop. For best results, use a flat-bottomed canner or pot that fits your burner.

Kitchen Tip

Keep your canning equipment organized and accessible by storing it on a rolling cart or in bins that can be pulled into place when you need them. It's so much easier to accomplish a canning session if you don't have to root around for your tongs, lid lifters, and funnels each time you want to put 'em up.

Q I have some really cute vintage utensils. Can I use those?

A Who doesn't love vintage? And when you are canning, it looks so sweet. I have a canning friend who has the most gorgeous enameled ladle that matches her canner. It's terrific.

If you have such items, they are usually fine to use. Just make sure that they are clean and rust-free. Avoid metals such as tin, iron, zinc, and copper, which can give your foods an off taste and dark color.

Q Are canning tongs the same as regular tongs?

A I used to think so. When I first started canning, I thought I could just substitute my regular tongs, wrapping the tips in rubber bands to make them grippier. I thought I was being frugal, but I was being foolish. Using anything but canning tongs to lift jars full of boiling-hot ingredients in and out of cauldrons of hot water is dangerous. Besides the jars, canning tongs are the one piece of equipment that you cannot do without!

Q Do I really need a canning funnel?

A I am a messy girl, so I find a canning funnel really helps me do a much neater job of loading my jars. But is it absolutely necessary? Absolutely not. You can just use a small ladle and try to be careful about your work — the less you spill on the rim of the jar, the less you have to wipe off before you center your lids on top.

Q I don't have a lot of canning equipment. Can I substitute anything?

A Preserving is an exercise in frugality and utility; it's about making the most out of what you have on hand. That includes the equipment you need to do it. The only two specialty items you need — things that can't be substituted with anything else — are canning jars and canning tongs. Using recycled all-purpose jars or cooking tongs can be dangerous. But everything else — the canner, rack, lid lifter, bubble tool, and funnel — you probably already have in your kitchen or can improvise out of something you own. Of course, if you can, it is nice to have a set of tools dedicated to the process. And if you want to pressure can, you will have to invest in a proper pressure canner. But otherwise, you can rig it up with things you already have in the kitchen.

Here is a list of swap-outs you can use to get canning.

- **Canner.** A pasta pot, lobster pot, or stockpot will make a fine canner. Any pot that can hold boiling water, is at least 3 inches taller than your biggest canning jar to allow for good water circulation, and has a tight-fitting lid can serve as a canner.

- **Canning rack.** A cake cooling rack or barbecue grill grate that is just a bit smaller than your canner or pot can be used as a canning rack. It should be flat to hold the jars level (a three-legged basket-style steamer rack fails on this measure). It should raise the jars off the bottom and have an open design so that the hot water can circulate all around. In a pinch, you can even lay down a single layer of canning jar rings to act as a rack. Do not use a kitchen towel on the bottom of the canner — it will not allow water to circulate under the jars.

Jar rings used as a canning rack

- **Lid lifter.** You can use silicone-tipped tongs or even your fingers to lift the lids out of the hot water. Just be sure not to use anything that might scratch the white undercoating of the lid in the process. A scratched lid can rust during storage, and you don't want that.

- **Bubble tool.** This tool removes trapped air from your filled jars before you seal them. You can use a chopstick, wooden skewer, or plastic knife to do the job. Just make sure not to use anything metallic that can scratch the glass and compromise the integrity of your jars, or they could crack during processing.

- **Funnel.** Canning funnels are handy for keeping things neat, but it isn't a deal breaker if you don't have one. You can saw off the bottom portion of a regular funnel to create a V-shaped cone that fits down into your jar. Or just use a small ladle and pour carefully.

Q What's a lid lifter?

A The lid lifter is another name for the magnet tool that is often included in a canning kit. It is essentially a magnet on a stick that you can use to retrieve washed and waiting lids one by one from their stack without burning your fingers in the hot water that is holding them. You can substitute a set of soft-tipped canning tongs or use your fingers to (quickly) grab the lids out of the hot water.

Q What kind of metal should my canner be made out of?

A Canners can be made out of any material that will hold boiling water. Any pot will do; enamel-coated aluminum is common, but you can use regular aluminum, stainless steel, or whatever you have. It just needs to be at least 3 inches taller than the tallest jar you are processing. A tight-fitting lid will help water come to a boil more quickly and prevent evaporation.

Q What is a nonreactive pot? Why is it important?

A A nonreactive pot is made of a metal that will not react chemically with your food. It's important to cook in a nonreactive pot so that your recipes won't pick up a metallic taste and your acidic ingredients won't corrode the inside of your pot. Stainless steel and enamel-coated cast iron are two popular types of cookware that are commonly used in preserving because they are nonreactive. Reactive cookware, such as aluminum pots, bowls, and spoons, will react with the highly acidic preparations suitable for the boiling-water method and should be avoided. One exception to the reactive rule is the use of copper confiture — specially designed, copper-lined pots for making sweet spreads. While copper is reactive, it can be used if strict cooking methods are employed to avoid leaching toxic metals into your recipe. (See page 189.)

Q My canner is rusting. Can I still use it?

A The most common canners are enamel coated to resist rusting, but through use, that coating can wear down, become scratched or dented, and leave the metal exposed and susceptible to rusting. A little spot of rust isn't harmful, but if there is enough decay to color your water, it's time to invest in a new canner. Keep in mind that rusted metal is weak metal. Rust spots can turn to holes at any time, and you don't want that time to be while you are processing (speaking from experience!).

To keep your pot rust-free, always wash it and dry it immediately after use. Keep in mind that adding vinegar to the water, as one does to avoid hard water staining on jars, will speed corrosion.

Jars

Q I saw some huge canning jars. What do you use a I-gallon jar for?

A The largest jar that is recommended for safe canning is the half-gallon size. It can only safely be used for canning apple or grape juice using the boiling-water method. It is not approved for any other canning use. (Be sure that your canner or pot is at least 3 inches taller than even this large jar to ensure good water circulation all around the jar.)

Such large-format jars are generally used for storage and decoration. I use mine for fermenting and making alcohol infusions, for which I appreciate the thick glass and roomy capacity.

Q Can I reuse canning jars?

A Yes! Use, use, and reuse. As long as the jars aren't chipped or scratched, you can keep on using them and pass them down for the next generation of canners. Unless they are bent or rusted, you can also reuse the bands.

However, the lids of the typical canning jars (those that are metal, with a white undercoating and a pink circle of sealant along the inside edge of the lid) are only good for one round of processing. After that, you can use them for storage, but they will not seal reliably.

If you are looking for an alternative, there is a line of reusable lids available. They are made of white plastic and come with pink rubber gaskets that look like flat rubber bands. These lids and their bands are reusable.

Kitchen Tip

Always mark your spent lids so that they don't get mixed up with new ones.

Q I have some gorgeous blue canning jars with zinc tops. Can I use those to can?

A I have some of those, too! They are lovely to have in the kitchen and are great for storing dry grains and odds and ends. Unfortunately, those jars are not reliable for safe canning. They just don't give the reliable seal of a two-piece lid.

Q I have some really pretty decorative jars. Can I use those to can?

A Decorative jars are terrific for storing and gifting infusions, provided that they are food-safe. They are not recommended, however, for canning. The glass is most likely too thin to withstand the process and, without a lid that vents and seals, you will not get the airtight seal that prevents contamination. For the best results, always use jars designated specifically for canning.

Q Can I use jars with rubber gaskets and clamps for canning? What about Weck jars?

A I will start by saying that the United States Department of Agriculture (USDA) does not recommend glass-top jars for canning. However, they are beautiful, and I know a number of home canners and chefs who use them to successfully put up acidic foods such as jams and jellies. To use these jars, you fill and process using the boiling-water method just as you would a standard two-piece-lid jar, but you need to apply the metal clamps to the lid to keep it in place during processing. Here are the pros and cons as I see them:

Pros

- No BPA. Because only glass touches your food, there is no exposure to Bisphenol A when using these jars.

- Less waste. You can reuse the jars and the lids as long as they aren't scratched or chipped. Only the rubber rings need to be fresh each time you can.

- Beauty. They look lovely on the shelf.

Cons

- Expense. The jars are pricey and can really add to the expense of home canning.

- Shipping. The jars are not made in the United States, so you will be adding shipping miles to your project.

- Ease of use. You have to apply the clamps to the hot, filled jars before processing. This can be tricky, and you have to protect your hands from the heat of the jars while doing so.

- Versatility. Although the company claims these types of jars are suitable for pressure canning, users report mixed results.

Q Can I use wire bail jars?

A Another kind of adorable jar, wire bail jars (which have a closure similar to those on Grolsch beer bottles), are not recommended for canning. While the locking mechanism is great for creating an airtight seal, it doesn't allow for the venting action that helps canning jars perform so well during processing. They are excellent for food storage. Use them to keep grains and meals dry and pest-free. And they are super cute, so you can enjoy their charm on the shelf.

Wire bail jars aren't for canning

Q How does jar size affect processing time?

A Proper processing ensures that heat fully penetrates to the core of the packed jars. This can happen much more quickly in a small jar than a large one, so processing times will reflect the specific vessel you are using. Filled half-pint jars, for example, will heat through well before a quart of the same recipe will reach temperature, so the processing time for the smaller jars can be less.

It's important to always follow the processing time indicated for your jar size. Insufficient processing (which can happen by using the processing time for a small jar when you are using a larger one) will leave the food at the center of the jar underprocessed. This can be a dangerous situation, as the contents at the center of the jar will not be cooked and may rot in storage, creating a hazardous product.

Conversely, overprocessing your jars (by using the processing time for a large jar when you are using a small one) can cause contents to leach out of the top of the jar, create pectin separation and/or dull flavors and textures. Always use the correct processing time indicated for the jar size you are using.

You also want to use only the jar sizes listed in the recipe. Canning recipes often offer a range. For example, "Process 8-ounce jars for 10 minutes, pints for 15." You shouldn't use jar sizes that are not listed in the recipe, as doing so may yield unsatisfactory results. Trying to process a quart of jam, for instance, could very well ruin the spread. It would be overprocessed in its outer layer before the heat ever reached the core of the jar. Use only the jar size indicated in your recipe.

Q How do I know whether to use regular- or wide-mouth jars?

A Technically, regular-mouth jars are designed to keep foods submerged under liquid. The curve of their shoulder is meant to prevent packed foods from bobbing to the top of the jar — sort of like a ledge that holds the packed food underneath. The straight neck is then supposed to contain a little extra liquid to ensure that your food remains covered with syrup or brine.

However, I don't find this design to be reliable enough to dictate the jar type that I use for my recipes. A well-packed jar is going to work, regardless of whether it has a regular or wide mouth.

I actually prefer the wide-mouth jars and use them exclusively in the pint and quart size. The wide mouth allows room for my big peasant hands to reach all the way in for easier packing and cleaning.

As long as you keep to the jar size indicated in your recipe, you can use either wide- or regular-mouth jars.

Q I have heard that there is BPA in the lids of canning jars. How can I avoid BPA in my canned foods?

A There is a lot of controversy over the possible health implications of exposure to BPA (Bisphenol A). At the time of this printing, many popular canning jars are phasing out the use of this compound in their lids. Some older jars use BPA in the white underside of the lid and cover it with a clear coating that keeps it from having contact with your food. While only lids that are BPA-free can guarantee zero exposure to the compound, the clear coating and the fact that canned foods have very little contact with the lid limit an eater's exposure. To further limit your exposure to BPA, follow these suggestions:

- Purchase recently manufactured jars.
- Always store your jars right-side up.
- Always maintain the amount of headspace indicated in the recipe.
- Never use scratched or dented lids.

There are also white plastic lids that can be used in place of the metal ones that come with the jars. They can be a little tricky to seal but are reusable and BPA-free.

Q Why do canning jars have two-piece lids?

A The most popular canning jars feature a two-piece metal top. The flat lid, the part of the top that covers the jar, is rimmed on the bottom with a gummy sealing compound that softens and forms to the jar's rim when heated and helps form a vacuum seal during processing and cooling. The flat lid is accompanied by the second piece of the top, a threaded ring that is lightly screwed on top of the jar to keep the lid in place during processing and cooling.

Because the lid has two pieces, it allows pressure to vent out of the top of the jar during processing. If you peek down into the water during the boiling-water method, you can see tiny bubbles escaping from the lid as soon as it is submerged. During cooling, the pressure reverses and the lid sucks down onto the jar, creating a vacuum and an airtight seal. You can hear the delightful *ping* the lids make when this happens — music to a canner's ears.

You can reuse the rings as long as they aren't rusted or bent, but the lids can be used for canning only once; after that they can be used for food storage, but the compound will never seal properly after being processed.

You may also see plastic replacement lids that use separate rubber gaskets that resemble a flat rubber band. These lids can be used instead of the flat metal lids that come with your jars. They act the same way as metal lids but need to be tightened after processing to form a vacuum seal. Many canners report that they have more seal failures with this type of lid. However, unlike the metal lids, they are reusable.

Q What is the best way to store jars between uses?

A Reusing jars makes canning much more economical than it would be if you had to buy new jars for each batch. It's important to keep them free of nicks and scratches that could prevent a good seal or cause the jars to break during processing. It's a good idea to keep the sectioned cardboard cases that the jars are sold in. As you empty the jars of their contents, you can wash them and place them, lid-side down to keep them from collecting dust, back in their original box. Between seasons, you might want to cover your jars to keep them from collecting dust by either storing them in a cabinet, wrapping them in paper, or sliding the whole case of jars inside an old pillowcase.

Q I like to pick up jars at yard sales. Is that okay?

A I am all for recycling, and jars are a great thing to reuse. You just have to be careful. Follow these tips to make the best of your bargain:

- Always check the rims of your jars for nicks. Even the smallest chip can prevent a good seal.
- Hold your jars up to the light and inspect for scratches. Scratched glass can shatter easily in the canner.
- Look at the rings. Make sure they aren't obviously rusted or dented. Be sure they twist onto the jars smoothly and without any hesitation.
- Lids should be in original packaging. You can use lids only once, so assume that any that are loose have already been used.
- If you can, inspect the lids to make sure that the sealing compound is fresh and pliant. Dried-out or cracked compound will not seal.

Process

Q I've never canned before. What's a good recipe to start with?

A Welcome to your new obsession! I've met so many eaters who held off on canning for years and the minute they jumped in became instantly hooked. Why not? It's pretty easy and very delicious.

If you have never canned before, the boiling-water method is the way to go. It's easy to get the hang of and doesn't require that you invest in any specialized equipment other than a set of tongs and the canning jars.

For recipes, I would start with pickles, such as classic Bread-and-Butter Chips (recipe, page 78). Pickles are easy and inexpensive to make, and there are so many varieties that you can make some kind of pickle almost anytime of year. All you need to remember to get a good pickle is to follow your recipe — use the type and amount of vinegar and produce indicated and they will taste great. Then you just dunk them down into the canner and process using the boiling-water method for the amount of time indicated in the recipe.

Once you have the boiling-water method under your belt and you are comfortable getting things into and out of the canner, you can move on to so many other recipes. Chutneys, relishes, and sauces are a great next step.

Many eaters start with jams and jellies. I don't recommend it. Not that they are terribly difficult — these sweet spreads use the same boiling-water method that all acidic recipes do. But it can take a little practice to get the right gel. So you might save them for your second or third time at the canner.

Once you're familiar with the boiling-water method, pressure canning will be an easy transition. You prepare and fill the jars the same way but the pressure canner — which seals tightly shut — traps steam to raise the jars' temperatures above the boiling point, so you can preserve nonacidic recipes.

Q What is headspace and why does it matter?

A Headspace is the distance between the top of the liquid in a filled canning jar and the top of the jar rim. Each recipe will indicate the amount of headspace required for that preparation. It can vary from ¼ inch for foods such as sweet spreads to up to 1 inch for items such as whole fruits.

headspace

Proper headspace is essential to a good seal. Too much headspace and there may be too much air for a sufficient seal. Too little headspace can cause the food to push up against the lid of the jar during processing, causing seepage and preventing a good seal. Always maintain the amount of headspace as it is listed in your recipe to achieve a good result.

With some canning experience, you will get a sense of what certain headspaces look like in the jar and you might be able to eyeball them accurately. But when you are first starting out, it's helpful to measure. It might seem over the top, but it's an easy way to remove one possible barrier to success. Some bubble tools come with a notched ruler on one end that allows you to measure your headspace. If you don't have such an implement, you can use a regular ruler. You might consider keeping a clean one in your kitchen just for this purpose. (It's also helpful for measuring cookie and pie dough thickness, so it's not entirely a single-use tool.)

Kitchen Tip

It's a good idea to keep a designated kitchen ruler handy for measuring headspace.

Q What does *fingertip-tight* mean?

A *Fingertip-tight* means just that — you use only your fingertips when tightening the lid. Using just your fingertips guarantees that you will tighten the lid just enough — secure enough that the lid has good contact with the rim of the jar but loose enough that the gases

BREAD-AND-BUTTER CHIPS

Makes about 7 pints

Easy, tasty, classic — that's Bread-and-Butter Chips. These delicious pickle slices are a must-have in any canner's repertoire. And they go so fast — on a burger or nestled next to a sandwich, on a cheese plate, or with a platter of charcuterie — that you might be wise to make a few batches. The recipe calls for resting the sliced cukes under a layer of ice for a time. Don't skip this step. The salt and ice refresh the produce and draw out excess moisture so you'll have a crisper pickle chip.

INGREDIENTS

- 5 pounds unpeeled cucumbers, ends removed, sliced into 1/4-inch coins
- 1 pound large onions, coarsely chopped
- 1/2 cup plus 1 tablespoon kosher salt
- 2 cups ice cubes
- 4 cups distilled white vinegar
- 2 cups water
- 1 cup sugar
- 2 tablespoons mustard seeds
- 1 tablespoon black peppercorns
- 1 tablespoon celery seeds
- 1 tablespoon ground turmeric

PREPARE

1. Layer the cucumbers and onions with ½ cup of the salt in a large bowl and cover with a layer of ice cubes. Set aside for 2 hours.

2. In a colander, drain and rinse the cucumber-onion mixture.

3. Combine the vinegar, water, sugar, mustard seeds, peppercorns, celery seeds, turmeric, and the remaining 1 tablespoon salt in a large saucepan and bring to a boil. Add the drained vegetables and return to a boil, stirring to ensure that all of the vegetables are heated through. Remove from the heat.

PRESERVE

Refrigerate: Ladle into bowls or jars. Let cool, cover, and refrigerate for up to 3 weeks.

Can: Use the boiling-water method (see page 95). Ladle into clean, hot pint jars, covering the pickles by ¼ inch with liquid. Leave ¼ inch of headspace between the top of the liquid and the lid. Use a bubble tool, or other nonmetallic implement, to release any trapped air. Wipe the rims, cover the jars, and screw the bands on just fingertip-tight. Process for 10 minutes. Cool for 24 hours. Check the seals and store in a cool, dark place for up to 1 year.

expelled during processing can be released and give you a good vacuum seal as they cool. Don't let your knuckles creep down the rim and never grip the lid and wrench it into place.

While it can be counterintuitive to put a jar with a lid that is not screwed on tightly down into a vat of boiling water, it is necessary to do so. Don't worry — you won't get salsa soup. The minute the jar is submerged under the boiling water, you will see tiny air bubbles start to rise from inside the jar. This outward pressure keeps any water in the canner from going inside the filled jars.

To know whether you have the correct tightness, place your filled jar down on your towel-covered surface. Place the lid on the jar and twist the ring on using just your fingertips, holding the jar lightly with your other hand. When the jar starts to spin from the grip of the ring, you are just about fingertip-tight. Given the opportunity, you could get nearly another quarter turn out of the jar, but you would be preventing the conditions necessary for getting a good seal. Just fingertip-tight. That's all you need!

Q Why is it important to remove all of the air bubbles from my jars before processing?

A It is not uncommon for air bubbles to get trapped in jars as you fill them, particularly when you are canning thick mixtures, such as chutneys, or whole fruits, which can trap air in the divot left by the pit or core when it was removed.

It is important to remove any trapped air in your jars before processing for a number of reasons. Most important, you want to ensure that you have the right amount of headspace. Any air that is trapped in your jar before processing will most likely rise to the top of the jar during processing, resulting in excessive headspace, which can lead to seal failure. Large air bubbles can also prevent brines and syrups from fully enveloping your food, which can lead to discoloration and possibly spoilage.

Always use a nonmetallic stick or skewer to dislodge any air trapped in your jars by running it between the food and the inside of your jar. Never use a metallic implement, which could scratch the glass. Top up the volume as necessary after removing air bubbles to achieve the proper headspace.

Q How long should my processed jars rest before I can store them?

A Give your jars a full 24 hours after processing before you move them. While they may cool to room temperature within a few hours, the extra time ensures that the seals completely firm up again.

If you think you might need your counter space before that time, you can transfer processed jars to a baking sheet covered with a tea towel. You can then move the whole sheet of jars to a quieter location while they rest. (See Workspace, page 58.)

Q Why do I need to wipe the rim of my jar before placing the lid on it? Doesn't this introduce bacteria to the jar?

A It's really important that the lid of your jar be completely free of any debris or sticky brine or syrup. Any little trapped seed or bit of food will prevent a good seal. Carefully wiping the lid is the only way to guarantee this. Use a fresh paper towel or clean tea towel that has been dipped in hot water to clean up your rim. Take your time and do it thoroughly. Any bacteria present will be destroyed during processing.

Q What is the difference between the hot-pack and cold-pack methods?

A The difference between hot and cold packing is simply a matter of whether the food is cooked or raw before it is loaded into your canning jars.

Salsas, jellies, jams, and chutneys are all cooked and, therefore, are hot-pack recipes. When preparing hot-pack recipes, it's important to move directly from the cooking process to the canning process, as the processing times for these recipes assume that the food will be piping hot when it is loaded into the jars. (The 5-minute rest that jams and jellies are sometimes given to set their gel will not cool them enough to impact your results.) Because the food is ladled into the jars cooked and hot, hot-pack recipes generally have shorter processing times.

cold-packed jar

Cold-pack foods are generally those that you want to organize in the jar nicely — such as asparagus or carrot spears — or those, such as apricots or tomatoes, that would fall apart into a sauce if cooked before being packed. Cold-pack recipes often call for the food to be covered with a hot brine or syrup. Careful attention to processing time ensures that the raw food will be heated through to the core of the jar during the canning process. These processing times can seem excessive, but are necessary to ensure that the food is completely cooked through. Never skimp on processing time or else cold-pack foods can remain raw and subject to rot during storage.

Q How tightly should I pack my raw vegetables into the jars for cold pack?

A You want to pack your jars so that they are full enough to keep the food from bobbing around but the produce isn't so tightly crammed in the jar that the brine or syrup cannot circulate. For firm vegetables, such as carrots and asparagus, the jar should be filled tightly enough that you could turn it upside down after packing (but before adding spices or ladling in brine) and not have the items fall out of the jar. Soft fruits should be gently compressed to fill air pockets as much as possible, without crushing or mashing. Be careful not to overfill cold-pack jars. It's not uncommon for the food to swell a bit under the heat of processing. Overfilled jars can push up against the lid of the jar and prevent a good seal.

Q Do I need to sterilize all of my equipment before using it to can?

A It is a common misconception that everything in the kitchen needs to be sterile for safe, successful canning. The truth is that a home kitchen will never be sterile. You don't need to scrub down with bleach or suit up in scrubs before you start.

Even if you were to try, you could get everything as germ-free as possible and then the dog sneezes in the corner and, well, it's just impossible to have a sterile kitchen. That's why modern canning methods, which kill any potentially contaminating bacteria after the jars are filled, give you the best possible outcome. Even if there are some lingering pathogens in the jar or in the air in the headspace, given sufficient processing, they will be destroyed by the heat of the water during boiling-water processing or the steam during pressure canning.

The only exception to this is the rare recipe that calls for the jars to be processed for under 10 minutes. This amount of time is insufficient to destroy any lingering bacteria. Therefore, for recipes that are processed for less than 10 minutes, yes, you do need to presterilize all equipment that will come in contact with your food by submerging it in boiling water for 10 minutes. That includes the jars, funnel, bubble tool, and ladle. The lids should be submerged in simmering water for at least 10 minutes but should not be boiled before processing, as doing so can oversoften the sealing compound and compromise the vacuum seal.

Q How do I know whether my jars have sealed correctly?

A It's easy to know if your jars have sealed. Just remove the ring, tip them upside down, and give them a good shake. If the food stays in the jar — you're there! It may sound silly, but it's a good test if you are nervous about how sealed is sealed. Try it over a bowl if you're leery of losing your pickles.

Too dramatic? Then just remove the ring and gently press up on the lid with your thumb. If the lid stays on the jar, you have a good seal. If it pops off easily, then your seal has failed. (But you haven't! Even the most experienced canner has a jar that doesn't seal once in a while. Just pop that one in the fridge and enjoy within 3 weeks.)

If you have a good seal, the jars are safe to store. Wipe your jars down and store them without their rings, which can trap moisture, in a cool, dark place for the time indicated in your recipe.

Kitchen Tip

Always write an opened-on date on your jars when you break the seal. That way you won't forget how long you have to enjoy your gorgeous creation.

Ingredients

Q Can I use iodized salt for canning?

A Iodized salt contains iodine, an element necessary for good health but not appropriate for canning. Iodine can discolor food or brine and give an off taste. Use salt that is free of any additives, such as pickling or kosher salt, for best results. (See A Glossary of Salt, page 55.)

Q I have hard water. How will it affect my canning?

A Hard water is highly mineralized water. Whether it is in your canner or in your jars will determine its impact on your results.

While hard water in your canner will not affect your food, it can leave a white haze on the outside of your jars. Add a few tablespoons of vinegar to your canning water to keep the mineral deposits from leaving this scaling on your canning jars.

The minerals in hard water can, however, affect your recipes. They can cause pickles to shrivel and give vegetables a tough texture. Iron and sulfur in your water will darken foods. If you have hard water, you may prefer to use distilled water in your recipes to avoid these ill effects. Alternatively, you can treat your hard water by boiling it, letting it settle for 24 hours, and carefully pouring off the softened water, leaving the sediment behind.

Hard water, while challenging to work with, is not harmful.

Q I have seen recipes that use food coloring, drink mixes, and even hard candy to change the color or taste of recipes. Is this safe?

A I am not a fan of using anything artificial in home food preservation (or any kind of cooking, really). Neon-colored pickles? Preserves flavored with Red Hots candy? Red dye in my apple slices? No thanks. There are lots of treated, altered, and otherwise doctored packaged foods on the grocery store shelves — no need to create your own.

One of the best reasons for preserving your own food is that you can control the ingredients, putting in only good things. Start with fresh, tasty, local food. Keep your food simple and let its delicious, natural flavors shine through.

Q Every time I get ready to preserve, I have to run to the store. What do you keep in a well-stocked canning pantry?

A Adding a store run on top of the time it takes to gather your food and set up can make home food preservation seem like so much more of a chore than it is. Keep the following items in your pantry and you will always be ready to jump right in.

The Canning Pantry

- Bottled lemon juice
- 5 pounds granulated white sugar
- 2 pounds brown sugar (light and dark)
- 1 box kosher salt
- Packets of pectin
- 1 gallon 5 percent white distilled vinegar
- 1 gallon 5 percent apple cider vinegar
- Fresh garlic
- Black peppercorns
- Assorted spices (Mustard seeds and celery seeds are commonly used in preserving recipes; cinnamon sticks, vanilla beans, and ground turmeric would not go to waste either.)

lemon juice

pectin kit

garlic

sugar

vinegar

spices

Kitchen Tip

When you are building your canning pantry, it's always useful to have a system in place to know when you need to replenish. Keep a checklist or, if you can, keep an extra of each item. When you are using your extra, you know it's time to restock.

Q Can I add liquid smoke to my canning recipes?

A I am not a fan of food additives, so I choose not to include them in my recipes. But if this is an ingredient that you enjoy, you can use it in your canned foods. Canning can intensify the flavor of liquid smoke, however, so you would be wise to use a light hand. Advocates say that one or two drops will get the job done.

When Something's Gone Wrong

Q When I open my jars, it smells like beer. Is that normal?

A Boozy smells indicate fermentation. Any odor of beer, wine, or whiskey is a sign that something has gone wrong. Perhaps your recipe contained insufficient acid or was not cooked or processed long enough. Discard it where no human or animal will accidentally consume it.

Q Why would my jar crack in the canner?

A The most common cause of cracking or breaking jars is a wide change in temperature. Putting cold jars into boiling water or setting your hot jars on a cold surface, for example, can stress the glass and cause breakage. Always avoid temperature extremes. Use tea towels to cover any surfaces that your hot jars will come in contact with. Never set hot jars directly on countertops, which can be quite cool, particularly if they are made of stainless steel or granite.

Any damage to the glass, no matter how small, can also cause it to crack in the canner. Examine your jars before using them for any hairline cracks or chips that could weaken the glass. Even new jars can arrive with tiny air bubbles that can lead to breakage in the boiling water. Metal utensils, particularly those with serrated edges, can scratch the glass. Be careful not to scrape the inside of your jars with metal utensils when removing air bubbles or serving up the contents of the jar.

Never use jars that are not intended for canning. Such jars will not have the thick glass that is necessary to withstand the high temperatures of the canning process. Be careful to maintain proper headspace and apply the lids just fingertip-tight. Pressure can build up in overfilled or overtightened jars and lead to seal failure and breakage.

Q The lids on my jars were tight when I put them on the shelves, but now they are popping off. What happened?

A Lids that bulge or pop off are a sure sign that something is wrong. Gas is being produced inside the jars, indicating an unstable environment. Perhaps your jars were not processed fully and there is now bacterial growth or your food is fermenting. Discard the contents of these jars immediately. The safest way to dispose of spoiled food is to boil it for 10 minutes and then discard it where no animal or human will accidentally eat it. Do not compost spoiled food.

Q If it smells good and it looks good, it's good, right?

A I wish I could say yes, but no. Some forms of contamination can be odorless and colorless. The only way to guarantee that your work is solid and your canned items are safe is to follow the recipe — never skimp on the acid or processing time, the two biggest causes of contamination.

Q What is siphoning?

A Siphoning is the loss of liquid from filled jars during or after processing. Some of the most common causes include the following:

- Overfilling jars, which prevents the lid from making good contact with the rim of the jar.
- Removing the jars from the boiling water too soon after processing.

- Artificially cooling a pressure canner by submerging it in cool water or packing cold towels around it.
- Screwing the band on too loosely.
- Leaving insufficient headspace.

To avoid siphoning, always:

- Let the jars rest in the hot water for 5 minutes after processing time has ended.
- Never force a pressure canner to cool.
- Apply your bands fingertip-tight.
- Allow the amount of headspace indicated in your recipe.

Q I processed my jars for longer than the recipe directed. Is it still okay to eat?

A Overprocessing can lead to *fruit float* (separation of liquids and solids in the jar), color and flavor loss, or mushy textures. It can also cause foods to leak out of the jar, affecting headspace. If the headspace has been maintained, you can eat overprocessed foods. Though they might be safe to eat, they could very well be unpleasant.

What Not to Do

Q I want to can my own baby food. Any pointers?

A Homemade baby food is great. Canning it, however, can be tricky. Puréed vegetables are hard to process thoroughly, leaving the little tyke at risk for contamination. And with babies' developing immune systems, even the slightest problem will be amplified. If you want to can food for the younger set, it's best to pressure can vegetables normally and then purée before serving. The USDA also recommends boiling such foods for 10 minutes and then cooling before serving to a baby.

Because they are acidic, puréed fruits are much less susceptible to contamination. You can confidently prepare puréed applesauce and pear sauce with a traditional canning recipe and have it on hand for the little one's lunch. The boiling-water method is sufficient for canning puréed fruits and is the technique of choice for such preparations.

Alternatively, baby foods can be frozen. You can purée anything that you'd like to put on the baby's plate — fruits, vegetables, even soups, stews, and moistened rice. Then ladle it into ice cube trays, cover, and freeze. You can transfer frozen cubes to sealable containers for long-term freezer storage or leave them in their covered trays. Individual cubes can be defrosted for easy baby-sized portions.

Q Can I can chocolate sauces?

A There are lots of recipes bouncing around the Internet for home-canned chocolate sauces. Of course, they sound very appealing — who wouldn't want to dig into Grandma's Homemade Fudge Sauce or Auntie Em's Raspberry Truffle Yum-Yum? They sound delicious and are often accompanied by some version of "been doing it for years and no one has gotten sick." Okay, maybe that's true, but as good as these recipes sound, I still wouldn't recommend them and neither does the USDA.

Chocolate has a high pH, so adding it to your recipe can make it unsuitable for the boiling-water method, which is appropriate only for acidic preparations. Even if you start out with a very canning-appropriate fruit-based jam, adding a bit of chocolate to it can easily shift it into a pH too high for the boiling-water method to handle. Chocolate's high fat content and thick consistency make it inappropriate for pressure canning as well. Adding chocolate to your recipes is just not a good idea.

I have seen a few recipes that pair cocoa powder with high-acid fruits, with claims that the powder doesn't affect the acid balance as much as does solid chocolate. I have made them myself and they taste great. But when I tested their pH, it hovered uncomfortably close to the 4.6 pH level that you need for food to be considered safe for canning. Perhaps I am just overly cautious, but I prefer a slightly bigger target than these recipes provide. I prefer to refrigerate or freeze these products rather than can them. They taste just as good stored that way and don't give me the heebie-jeebies from having a borderline pH.

Q Can I can recipes with oil in them?

A Canning recipes with a high proportion of oil in them are not recommended for the boiling-water method or pressure canning. Oil is a nonacidic liquid that can easily trap bacteria and allow it to proliferate. The USDA warns strongly against canning any recipe, such as pesto or vinaigrette, that has a significant amount of oil in it. While I am no government wonk, I do tend to err on the side of caution, so I don't can oily recipes either.

That being said, there are long-held traditions of preserving food under oil that fly in the face of the rules and have fed eaters for millennia. I use this rule: If you learned your food preservation traditions from an experienced practitioner — if your *nona* or *abuela* took you by the hand and taught you how, or if you traveled far and wide to learn at the side of someone in possession of generations of knowledge about off-the-beaten-track methods — terrific. There is nuance and craft that can be passed down hand to hand that can't be captured any other way. I would never stand in the way of cultural tradition.

However, if you are just feeling your way through this thing, then stick to the path that will give you the widest margin for error. At least until you book that ticket to Italy.

Q I have a recipe that calls for alum. What is that?

A Alum is a firming agent used in recipes for fermented pickles. It has no effect on vinegar pickles. It can be found in the spice section of many supermarkets. Even though you can find it right next to the cinnamon, it is a corrosive chemical that needs to be handled with care. It can cause skin irritation and also cause vomiting or even death if ingested in sufficient amounts. Perhaps because of these dangers, alum has fallen out of favor with modern cooks.

In lieu of alum, you can get a crisper pickle by slipping a few oak, cherry, or grape leaves into the crock. The tannins in them will keep your produce sturdy. And always cut off at least ¼ inch of the blossom end of your cucumbers. These ends contain enzymes that can soften your produce as it ferments.

Q I have some great recipes for dips. Can I can them?

A As much as we might like to think that with enough processing time we could can anything, vegetable dips are not good candidates for the craft. Neither the boiling-water method nor pressure canning is suitable for any kind of dairy-based recipe. Dairy fats such as cream, butter, and cheese can alter the penetration of heat into foods, creating a dangerous, botulism-friendly environment. And dairy just doesn't perform well in the jar, where the heat tends to curdle and separate milk fats.

Q What about canning powders or aspirin? Can I add those to my recipes to make them safe?

A Canning powders and aspirin will not make your food safe to eat. There are no additives that, used alone, will make for safe canning. While there are a number of powders that are used in the process of canning, the proper boiling-water method or pressure-canning procedures must be followed to achieve a shelf-stable product. Here are some of the most common powders that are used in home canning and their role in the process:

- **Calcium powder,** found in some pectin kits, is used in conjunction with the pectin to achieve a gel.
- **Citric acid** acidifies recipes such as whole canned tomatoes.
- **Pectin powder** helps jams achieve their gel.
- **Canning salt** is a fine-grain salt that is used in brine making for its ability to dissolve quickly.
- **Calcium chloride** is a crisping agent used in pickle making. It is also available under the brand name Pickle Crisp.
- **Clear Jel** is a commercial thickening agent used to give body to relishes.

Q Can I process my jars by inserting them into my compost heap?

A Although a good compost heap can get pretty hot, it is not recommended as a safe way to process your canned foods. I applaud your good pile and am sure it is going to be great for many uses. Canning is not one of them.

Q Can I can butter?

A Canning is not recommended for dairy products. The fat in them does not perform well in the heat of the process. Butter is, in fact, already an example of home food preservation in its own right. It's a way to store milk fat for an extended time. This is particularly effective when the butter is *cultured,* inoculated with lactic bacteria, so that it propagates its own lactic acid.

While canning is not a good fit for extending the life of dairy, fermentation is. Yogurt and cheese are just a couple of the products that use fermentation to extend the life of animal milk products. And they do it deliciously.

Q I have a vacuum bag sealer that allows me to make boil-in-bag foods. Can I preserve my foods this way?

A These bags might be great for getting an airtight seal on refrigerated and frozen foods, but they are not safe for preserving food that is destined to be stored on the shelf. Even though you can create an airtight environment and drop the bag into the boiling water, this method is not the same as processing your jars. Undetermined pH levels and processing times are two of the main reasons this is a risky proposition.

While you may see commercially prepared boil-in-bag foods on the grocery shelf, these are not examples that the home cook can follow. Such products are cooked and sealed using methods that are not available for home use. Always follow proven canning methods and recipes for preserving food at home.

Storage

Q Where should I store my processed jars?

A It is natural to want to show off all of those gorgeous jars of food. You have worked so hard and they look so good. Resist the temptation to put them on display, however, as exposure to light and heat will affect their quality negatively. Such conditions can cause colors to fade and, in the worst (and hottest) case scenario, seals to fail.

For best results, you should store your jars in as cool and dark a place as possible. A dry place would be even better. A basement is ideal, as long as it isn't too damp. But the back of a closet, behind the couch, or under the bed are okay substitutes if you are an apartment dweller. Any place that doesn't get a lot of light and has minimal temperature fluctuations is what you want. If you can't find a dark place, you can wrap your jars individually in paper or store them in a covered box.

Avoid storing canned foods in the kitchen, where there is usually a fair amount of light and where temperatures can swing widely, particularly at heights. The high shelf on the kitchen rack where beams of sunlight radiate through your blushing apricots may show off your jars the best but will ruin your food. It's fine if you want decoration, but not great if you want a good meal. Store your goods away; then they can have their dramatic debut come suppertime.

Kitchen Tip

Always store your jars without the rings. Humidity from the air or any lingering residue from the canning process that is trapped between the lid and a ring can lead to rust of one or both pieces and cause seal failure. Storing the jars without the rings on prevents moisture from building up around the lid.

Q My filled jars have mold on the outside. Should I pitch them?

A If you store your jars in a very damp area, such as a basement, they can sometimes harbor mold on the outside of the jar. This is usually caused by a bit of residue on the outside of the jar that didn't get cleaned off before storage. Mold has a way of working its way under a seal, given the chance. So inspect any moldy jars carefully. If you don't see any indication that the mold has worked its way under the jar — if your seal is still very tight when you open the jar, and you see no sign of mold on the food or on the inside of the lid or jar — your food is safe to eat. If you see any sign that the mold has infiltrated the seal, discard immediately.

To avoid mold growth on the outside of your jars, always wash them thoroughly before storage. If you see any mold forming, wash it off immediately, before it has a chance to compromise your seal.

Q My canned food froze in storage. Can I eat it?

A Canned food can freeze if left in an exposed part of the basement, such as near a storm door. If you know that your food has frozen, check the seals. If the seal is intact and you do not see any cracks or damage to the jars, then you can eat the food. The freezing and defrosting process may have softened the texture of the food but will not compromise its safety unless the seal has been damaged.

Q How long will the food keep after I process it?

A Most canned food is shelf stable for up to 1 year. You can best preserve the color and texture of your canned items by storing them in a cool, dark place. But I have friends in Brooklyn who don't have a basement and store their goods under their beds and in the back of their closets with fine results. After a year, all home-canned food will begin to lose quality.

Kitchen Tip

Always write the name of the recipe and the made-on date on your jar lids in permanent ink after you process them. Tied-on tags are great for gift giving but often come off in storage, leaving you to guess at the jars' contents.

Q My mother has some jars on her shelf that she canned 2 to 3 years ago. Are those still good?

A Home-canned foods can have flavor, and they can have stories, but they should not have vintages! Unlike wine and women, they do not get better with age. Most canned items should be enjoyed within a year. After that, color and flavor will fade. Seals can also dry out and loosen over time, creating an unsafe product. If you find yourself with a surplus of canned goods at the end of their shelf life, throw a pickle party or jam-off to empty out your (reusable) jars and make room for a new season's worth of tasty eating.

CHAPTER 5

Boiling-Water Method

The boiling-water method is the most popular method for home food preservation. If you can boil water, you can do this process. It's that simple. The only, very important, cannot-stress-it-enough thing to know about the boiling-water method is that it is only to be used for *acidic* recipes. That includes a lot — all of your jams, jellies, chutneys, relishes, salsas, whole tomatoes, whole fruits, and pickles can be canned with this method. But it is *not* appropriate for vegetables without added acid (such as green beans in water, corn in water, and so forth) or meat, fish, or recipes that contain animal protein or tofu. (For example, you will find boiling-water method recipes for tomato sauce, but you cannot use the boiling water method for tomato sauce with meat.) You don't need to measure your pH to get it right; just follow your recipe and all will be fine. Canning recipes that use the boiling-water method are carefully tested to ensure that the balance of acid to produce is just where it needs to be for safe and delicious results. Follow your recipe (and the tips in this book) to canning success!

Basics

Q I hear that this process is pretty easy. Can you just run me through the basics?

A Yes, if you can boil water, you will be able to can a lot of your own food. The boiling-water method is safe for all acidic recipes, so with it you will be able to put up jam, jelly, salsa, relish, chutney, pickles, whole tomatoes and fruit, and more. Here's how it works.

1. **Wash your equipment.** You don't need to use any special cleansers, but it's important that all of your equipment be clean. Wash everything in hot, soapy water and arrange on a clean tea towel. Wash your canner and rack and set it on a burner. Separate your jars into their three components and wash them up, placing the lids in a small heatproof bowl.

Loaded Canner

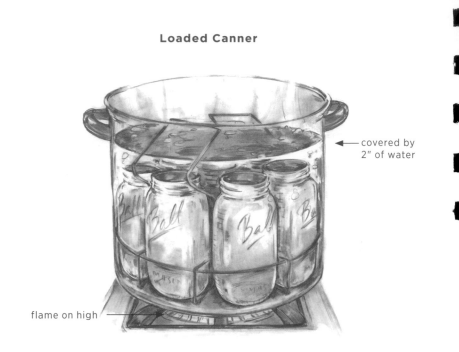

covered by 2" of water

flame on high

2. **Load your canner.** Place the jars, open-side up, on top of the rack in your canner. Make sure you have a full layer of jars, even if you are just going to process a few. Fill the canner and jars with cold water until all the jars are submerged. Turn the heat on high and cover your canner.

3. **Prepare your recipe.** Now is the time to cook your recipe. You never want your recipe to wait for your canner to heat up. Get it going now so it will be ready and waiting when your recipe is through.

4. **Fill the jars.** Using canning tongs, remove a jar from the canner, pouring the hot water inside it over the lids in the heatproof bowl. Remove the remaining jars for your recipe,

Softening the seals

Filling the jars   Removing air   Cleaning the rims
                      bubbles

tipping the water inside of them directly back into the canner. Using a canning funnel or a small ladle to prevent spills, gently fill the jars to the headspace recommended in your recipe. Use a bubble tool or other nonmetallic instrument to swipe the insides of the jar and release any trapped air. Wipe the rims with a damp paper towel. Center the lids on the jars. Screw the bands on just fingertip-tight.

5. **Process the jars.** Using canning tongs, load the jars into the canner. Make sure that you have at least 2 inches of hot water covering the jars. Place the cover on the canner and bring to a rolling boil. Process for the amount of time indicated in the recipe. When the processing time is over, turn off the heat, remove the lid from the canner, and let the jars rest for 5 minutes. Using canning tongs, lift the jars straight out of the canner, being careful not to tip them, and set on a towel-covered surface to rest for 24 hours.

Loading the canner

6. **Remove the rings and check the seals.** Remove the jar rings and push up gently but firmly on each lid; if the lid stays in place, you have a good seal. Thoroughly wipe the jar and lid with a clean tea towel to remove any residual moisture. Store the jars without their rings, which can trap moisture and jeopardize your seal. Properly sealed jars can be stored in a cool, dark place for up to 1 year.

Testing the seal

Q I have an old steam canner. Can I use that instead of the boiling-water method?

A Steam canners became popular in the 1970s but have fallen out of favor since then. They don't provide the safe, consistent results that you get using the boiling-water method or a pressure canner. I still see them gathering dust on the shelves of some hardware stores and wonder why they still carry them. The USDA does not recommend canning with a steam canner, and I don't know anyone who uses one. Processing times for the boiling-water method and pressure canning are specific to those processes and cannot be applied to the steam method.

Q Can I can outside?

A It can be difficult to maintain constant heat for pressure canning, but it's fine to use the boiling-water method outside as long as the breeze isn't strong enough to keep your pot from boiling. I love to can outside, and I have assembled an inexpensive and efficient setup to help me do it. I use a folding table for prepping and a two-burner propane camp stove to cook on. Canning this way can be much cooler than processing in a kitchen, which can become quite steamy over the course of a day of preserving. And cleanup is a breeze — just give the area a good hose-down when you are done.

Even if you want to do just part of the process in the open air, an outdoor picnic table or folding table is a terrific place to work. Messy jobs such as shucking corn and pitting cherries are great to take outside, where you can leave the mess behind. And tedious efforts, such as extensive chopping and dicing, are made much lighter when done gathered around a picnic table under a shady tree.

No matter where you are working, it's important that all of your surfaces be clean and tidy. You might want to cover prepped food with a tea towel to keep bugs from settling in for lunch. But a sterile environment is not the goal — fresh air and sunshine are terrific sanitizers and make for a fine place to work.

Q How do I keep the water from boiling off during processing?

A To start, you should always have at least 2 inches of boiling water covering your jars. This not only ensures that they will be completely surrounded by very hot water, but it also gives a little margin so your water doesn't boil down below your jars during processing. Keeping a lid on your canner will minimize water loss during processing, so always put one in place. For recipes that process for an extended amount of time, such as whole tomatoes, which can process for more than an hour, keep a kettle of boiling water at the ready so you can top off your canner if need be.

If, during processing, the water level falls below the top of the jars, you will need to replenish the water so that it is covering the jars by 2 inches and start the processing time over again.

Setting Up

Q Why do you put your lids in a small bowl of hot water before canning?

A Putting your lids in a small bowl of hot water before processing gives the gaskets a chance to limber up. The hot water softens the pink compound that edges the lid, providing it a better opportunity to conform to the rim of the jar and giving you a better chance of getting a strong seal.

Q Why do you fill the canner with cold water? Wouldn't hot water be faster?

A While canning jars are very strong, they are not invincible. One of their weaknesses is large swings in temperature. Excessive temperature changes can shock the glass, causing it to shatter. You would never want to load room temperature jars into boiling water — it's too abrupt a shift for the glass. Always load cool jars into cool water. Conversely, you want to make sure that you are loading jars freshly filled with piping-hot ingredients into hot water.

Q Why do you arrange all of your equipment on kitchen towels? Isn't the counter just as good?

A It's important to have several clean tea towels on hand for your canning session. Here are a few ways that they will help you out:

- **Cleanliness.** While canning isn't a sterile process, it should be a clean one. Laying down a clean towel will give you a nice new surface on which to arrange your freshly washed equipment.

- **Water.** Canning is a wet process. That towel will also catch the excess water to make the process a bit less sloppy and soppy. Not only will it keep the moisture to a minimum, but the towel's absorbency will also keep your jars from hydroplaning in the puddles of water on the counter.

- **Breakage.** Any abrupt change in temperature — from hot to cold or vice versa — can shock the glass and cause it to crack. The towel provides an important barrier between your hot jars and your cool countertop. This is particularly important on stainless or granite countertops, which can be chilly.

For all the same reasons, it's helpful to have a tea towel laid out and ready to receive your processed jars.

Q Why do I have to fill my canner with jars if I am going to be processing only a few?

A Loading your canner with a full layer of jars ensures that they will not fall over during processing. This is important because the seals are not formed until well after processing — after they have been removed from the canner and allowed to cool for 24 hours. If the jar tips before it has sealed, either during processing or when being lifted into or out of the canner, it can easily leak its contents, increasing headspace and keeping a good seal from forming.

However, while you do need to have a full layer of jars, they don't need to be the same size as the ones you are using in your recipe. If you are processing 8-ounce jars, for example, you can fill any extra space with quarts. Just make sure they are arranged snugly enough to keep everything vertical.

Q Why do you start your canner and then cook your recipe? Shouldn't it be the other way around?

A Canners contain a great quantity of water that, depending on the power of your cooktop, can take a surprisingly long time to come to a boil. So you want to give it all the time it needs to come up to heat before your recipe is ready to be canned.

You never want to go the opposite way and have your recipe waiting for the water in your canner to come to a boil. Doing so can cause recipes such as sweet spreads to thicken in the pot, making it hard to get a good pack. Most important, the processing times indicated in your recipes are developed with the assumption that the food or brine is piping hot when loaded into the jars. If these foods are cool when you fill the jars, the processing time may be insufficient to heat the contents to the core.

If your canner comes to a boil before your recipe is ready, simply cover it and turn off the heat. It will stay very hot for a good, long time. Then, when your recipe is ready, just crank the heat back up again and you can quickly resume your boil.

Q There are a lot of different size canners on the market. How do I know which one is for me?

A First of all, ask yourself whether you need to buy a canner at all. If you have a lobster pot or pasta pot that is 3 inches taller than your largest jar and that has a lid, this may be all you need, particularly if you are just starting out or don't see yourself canning much more than a few jars a year. If you think that canning is something you would really like to get into or if you will be processing jars that are too tall for your tallest pot, then you might consider purchasing a dedicated pot that suits your canning needs. Think about the kinds of foods you like to can. If you do a lot of jams and jellies, you might want a smaller canner. It will heat up quickly and still have enough room for the 4- and 8-ounce jars that those spreads are sealed in. If you think you might do more pints — things like pickled vegetables and salsas, for example — then you might want to get a canner with a slightly larger capacity. And if you want to can quarts of tomatoes or other whole fruits, then you want to invest in one of the larger canners. They can be cumbersome, but if you want to do decent-size batches of quart jars, then they are worth the expense and storage space. (See Canning Equipment, page 64.)

Q Can I just use my old mayonnaise jars for the boiling-water method?

A Recycling is such a smart idea, and there are tons of things that you can do with old mayo jars, but canning is not one of them. The glass jars that are used for retail food sales aren't designed to withstand the high temperature changes that are part of canning, and they could very well crack or shatter during the process. Additionally, they lack the two-piece lid that allows the airtight seal to form, which could lead to spoilage. For all food processing, specially designed three-part canning jars are best.

Q Do I have to sterilize my jars before I fill them?

A Not for most recipes. But do notice that I said *most*. You will occasionally come across a canning recipe that calls for a very short processing time. For any recipe that has less than 10 minutes of processing time, you must presterilize your jars and all equipment that will come in contact with your food by submerging it in boiling water for 10 minutes. Keep the jars submerged until ready to fill.

Q Can I heat my jars in the oven to sterilize them?

A Sterilization is necessary only for recipes that are processed for less than 10 minutes. Sterilizing your jars in your canner is the easiest and most efficient way to accomplish this, and it's foolproof. You will need a canner full of boiling water for processing anyway, so it's already available to you. Submerge the jars under 2 inches of water, bring it to a boil for 10 minutes, turn off the heat, and keep them there until you are ready to proceed with the recipe. While heating your jars in the oven might get them hot enough to sterilize them, you will have to pull racks of very hot, heavy glass jars out of the oven — a dangerous prospect in itself.

About pH and Acid

Q What is the pH that is safe for the boiling-water method?

A Foods processed using the boiling-water method must have a pH of 4.6 or less to be shelf stable. Foods with a higher pH (such as vegetables without any added acid, meat, fish, or recipes that contain meat or fish) may harbor pathogens that are not destroyed at the boiling point and must be processed using a pressure canner. You don't need to test for pH; just follow a tested recipe. Modern canning recipes are carefully developed to have the right balance of acid, in the form of vinegar, lemon juice, or the natural acidity of the fruit, for the proportion of produce in the recipe. To maintain the proper pH of your recipe:

- *Never* reduce the amount of acid in the recipe.
- *Never* increase the amount of produce in the recipe.

Q What kinds of acids are used in home food preservation?

A Acid is the key to successful home food preservation. Any food preserved using the boiling-water method must have a pH of 4.6 or less. Acid also acts as an anti-browning agent and promotes formation of a good gel. Following are some of the kinds of food acids that play a role in home food preservation:

Ascorbic acid, also known as vitamin C, is used in home food preservation as an anti-browning agent. It is available in crystal form or as tablets. Each teaspoon of the crystals contains about 3,000 mg of ascorbic acid, the equivalent of six 500 mg tablets. The crystals or crushed tablets are mixed with water to create an acid bath that protects the color of fruits such as apples, apricots, peaches, and pears.

When my recipe calls for both blanching and an acid bath (in recipes using peaches, for example), I often combine the two processes by adding ascorbic acid to my ice bath. It saves space, time, and cleanup. Blanched fruit goes into the acidulated ice bath to cool and is then peeled and returned to the same bath to seal its color.

Citric acid plays an important role in home canning: it is used to lower the pH of recipes to below 4.6 so that they can safely be preserved with the boiling-water method. Often such recipes call for either citric acid, available in powder form, or lemon juice; the two can be used interchangeably to achieve the same effect. Never reduce the amount called for in a recipe because, even though you may not be able to taste it, it is a critical element in safe home food preservation.

Citric acid can also be used as an anti-browning agent, though it is not as effective as ascorbic acid.

Lemon juice contains both ascorbic and citric acid, but in lower concentrations than the powdered and crystal forms. While it doesn't pack the acidic punch of ascorbic and citric acid powders, it offers terrific flavor that can bring an essential brightness to your preserves, particularly for long-cooking spreads that can dull in flavor during their time on the stove.

Acetic acid is the pucker power you find in vinegar. It can be an important element in a recipe destined for the boiling-water method, as it can effectively lower the pH to a level safe for canning. However, its strong flavor means that it will always play more than a supporting role, as it often dominates the flavor of the preserve. This can be used to great effect in making pickles, of course, and when balanced with sugar and other flavorings, acetic acid can make for great-tasting chutneys and sweet-sour pickled fruits, such as pickled plums.

Lactic acid is created during fermentation. Essentially, it is controlled rot. It might sound off-putting, but it tastes delicious! Fresh produce is submerged in a brine; the salt keeps pathogens at bay while beneficial bacteria act on the fruits and vegetables, digesting their sugar and converting it to lactic acid, which gives the food the acidic pH that keeps it safe on the shelf.

Q Can I use litmus paper to test my pH?

A Litmus paper is fine for testing the pH of your garden soil so that you can amend it properly. However, it is not recommended for use in home canning. Safe canning relies on a very precise pH level that cannot be captured by the litmus slips. Follow only approved recipes for home food preservation. If you want to can a home-designed recipe, contact your local ag extension for facilities in your area that can help you test the safety of your product.

Q Can I just use fresh lemon juice? Why do I have to use bottled?

A The bottled versus fresh lemon juice smackdown — it's been a steady debate among canners for some time. There are fans of fresh lemon juice who swear by it and use it all the time with very good results. I use bottled for a number of reasons. The acidic pH of bottled lemon juice — which is why we use it in canning in the first place, for its acid — is more consistent than that of individual lemons. I also have limited access to organic lemons but can find preservative-free, additive-free organic lemon juice quite easily. If I don't use the whole bottle, I can fill an ice cube tray with juice and have preportioned frozen lemon juice on hand all the time.

Q I love organic vinegar that has the mother in the bottom of the bottle. Why can't I use that?

A You can, but you will wind up killing your mother, so to speak. The high temperatures of brine preparation and the boiling-water method itself will kill the living probiotic organisms that are one of the primary benefits of enjoying such vinegar. If you still wish to use unpasteurized, organic vinegar in your recipes, it's safe to do so as long as it has been diluted to 5 percent acidity, a claim that will be clearly detailed on the label.

Q Can I use homemade vinegar in my recipes?

A Homemade vinegar is delicious, but its pH can vary. Canning recipes are developed for 5 percent vinegar, and you have no way to know if your homemade brew is packing enough acid to do the job. Save your homemade vinegar for refrigerator pickles, where refrigeration helps the vinegar preserve the food and acidity isn't as critical.

Q Can I use rice wine vinegar in my canning recipes?

A It is imperative that any vinegar you use in your canning recipes have 5 percent acidity — this fact will be clearly noted on the label. So let that be your guide. You can substitute different vinegars — white distilled, apple cider, malt, and so forth — as long as you are sure they pack the acidic power necessary to keep your recipes reliable. Keep in mind, though, that the flavor and color of the vinegar will affect your final results — sometimes in a good way, but sometimes it can just make them a bit funky.

Q Can I substitute apple cider vinegar for distilled white vinegar?

A You can substitute apple cider vinegar for distilled white vinegar as long as it has a 5 percent acidity (it will say as much on the label). Keep in mind that the living "mother" that is found in some unpasteurized vinegars, while great when consumed raw, will lose its probiotic nature when heated. Beware of vinegars labeled "apple cider flavored." These vinegars have been altered with natural or artificial flavorings that may act poorly in your recipe.

Q Can I use red wine vinegar in my recipes?

A Any vinegar that is diluted to 5 percent acidity is safe to use in canning recipes. You can replace white distilled vinegar with apple cider vinegar or even red wine vinegar as long as the label indicates it is diluted to 5 percent acidity. But keep in mind that deeply flavored vinegars will affect your results by changing the color and flavor of your produce. Red-tinged carrots might look pretty, but pink cucumbers may not appeal. Intensely flavored vinegars such as malt and balsamic vinegars can overpower your recipe if used in any quantity.

Q I just processed a batch of salsa and then realized that I used 4 percent acidity vinegar. What can I do?

A Unfortunately, your recipe will come up a bit short in the acidity department. You can't swap out 5 percent vinegar for 4 percent and get the same results. The altered recipe would have to be tested to know if the pH was low enough for safe canning. You have two options. You can refrigerate the salsa and enjoy it as it is, within a few weeks. Or you can contact your local ag extension and see if they will test the pH of the salsa to check whether it is safe to store. Always use the kind and amount of acid indicated in your recipe for safe results.

Reliable Recipes

Q My yield is different from what's indicated in the recipe. Did I do something wrong?

A Canning yields can vary from batch to batch. Even though canning is a fairly precise process, the ripeness of your food and size and shape of your pot can all lead to some variation. One batch of jam from very ripe fruit might need to cook a bit longer to get it to gel — so it will reduce a bit. You might make one batch of pickles in a high-sided pot and another in a low-sided vessel, each of which will contribute to a varying degree of evaporation during the process.

If the variation in your yield is minimal — within 10 to 20 percent — all should be fine. However, if you find that your yield is very different from the recipe — say, half as much or twice as much — I would review the process to make sure you didn't miss a step. Perhaps you left out an ingredient? Maybe you added the vinegar but left out the water sometimes called for in a brine? And if you left out the sugar in a jam recipe (unlikely, as it's often so important to the gel), it will be quite easy to recognize.

To guard against accidentally leaving something out, or losing count and adding less of an ingredient than you should, it's a good idea to lay out all of your ingredients ahead of time. This *mise en place*, as it is called, not only makes for smooth work at the stove, but it is also an easy way to make sure that everything makes it into the pot. To set your mise en place, measure out all of your ingredients ahead into appropriately sized dishes and add them as your recipe dictates.

Alternatively, you can check off your ingredients as they go into the pot so that any interruptions (or a wandering mind, in my case) won't take your recipe off course.

It's also a good idea to make sure you have an extra jar loaded into your canner in case you have a slightly bigger yield than expected. Keep partially filled jars covered and in the refrigerator and enjoy your goodies soon; most canning recipes can be refrigerated for several weeks.

Q Can I substitute fresh herbs for dried herbs in my recipes?

A Fresh herbs have a more delicate flavor than dried, so you will not get the same results by substituting one for the other. The flavor of fresh herbs tends to fade quickly during cooking, and by the time you cook and process, you will have a shadow of the taste they can offer if cooked more quickly. If your recipe calls for fresh herbs, add them just at the end of cooking in order to retain as much of their fresh-from-the-field flavor as possible. Dried herbs, on the other hand, tend to release flavors over time, so the long cooking process actually coaxes out the volatile oils that flavor the pot.

Additionally, by substituting fresh herbs for dried, you can risk throwing off your acid balance. If you load up your recipe with more produce than is called for in the ingredient list, you can quickly lower the acidity of the recipe. Add fistfuls of fresh vegetal matter in place of the relatively small amount of dried herb that is generally called for in a recipe and that's just what you are doing.

Q I love spicy food. Can I add hot sauce to my recipes to turn up the heat?

A While altering recipes is discouraged, this is one of the rare exceptions. Because bottled hot sauces are vinegar-based, they can be safely added to a recipe without lowering its acidity. You can also add ground dried chiles, such as ground cayenne or ancho peppers, to your recipes to increase the punch they pack.

Q Can I increase the amount of spices in my recipes?

A While it is never a good idea to alter a canning recipe, you can swap out one spice for another. If your recipe calls for cinnamon and you prefer nutmeg, it's fine to substitute one dried spice for another. It's one way to put your personal stamp on your canned items without risking the results.

And you can, within reason, add a bit more of a powdered spice or a few more peppercorns if you like. If your chutney calls for a tablespoon of ground dried chiles and you would rather turn up the flavor, you can safely add another tablespoon and be within the bounds of safety. Now, whether your taste buds can handle that amount of oomph is entirely up to you.

Q I've noticed that most recipes call for whole black peppercorns instead of ground pepper. Can I substitute ground spices for whole in my recipes?

A Whether your spices are whole or ground can really alter their impact on a recipe. First, whole spices often pack more flavor than packaged ground spices. The oils that make spices so tasty start to oxidize and lose their punch as soon as they are ground and sometimes can have a musty flavor if left too long on the shelf — something you don't want to impart to your recipes.

Second, ground spices are more likely to cloud your recipes. Sometimes, this is unavoidable. If you have ever made bread-and-butter pickles, you'll notice that the ground turmeric that is essential to this recipe can sometimes give the pickling liquid a cloudy appearance, sort of like sand shaken in a jar of water. Yet, the pickles wouldn't taste the same without it. So it's one instance where a powdered spice is the only option, even if it does cause some clouding.

And last, sometimes you want that flavor in the brine, but you don't want it to coat every piece of food. Staying with the bread-and-butter pickles example, it's nice to have the hint of heat that the peppercorns bring to the brine, but I wouldn't want a pickle chip speckled with bits of ground pepper in every bite. On the flip side, a jam, such as cherry with black pepper, greatly benefits from the addition of ground pepper rather than peppercorns, which would be a shocking surprise to bite into and therefore inappropriate in a spread.

The form of spice listed in your recipe is most likely specified for a reason. We recipe writers are kind of prickly about specificity. That being said, you can swap out whole for ground spices if you need or want to. If, for example, the recipe calls for a whole cinnamon stick and you don't have that on hand, you can add a bit of ground cinnamon instead. Your recipe won't be the same, but it will still be tasty.

PICKLED OKRA

Makes about 4 pints

I have taken some heat from my southern friends for not having a recipe for pickled okra in previous books. Well, here you go, y'all.

Cold packing the okra pods makes it easier to arrange them prettily in the jar. And let me tell you, there aren't many things as pretty as a jar of pickled okra on the shelf. Remove the seeds and ribs from the chiles if you want to decrease the heat level.

INGREDIENTS

2 red chiles, such as ripe jalapeños, halved lengthwise, seeds and ribs removed, if desired

2 cloves garlic, sliced

4 pounds okra, stems trimmed to ¼ inch long

1 teaspoon dill seeds

1 teaspoon black peppercorns

3 cups water

3 cups distilled white vinegar

1 tablespoon kosher salt

PREPARE

1. Divide the chiles and garlic among 4 clean, hot pint jars. Pack in the okra, alternating stem- and blossom-side up. (It can help to lay your jar on its side to get a good, straight pack.) The produce should be wedged in tightly enough that you can turn the jar upside down and the produce will not fall out. Divide the dill seeds and peppercorns among the jars.

2. Bring the water and vinegar to a boil in a small saucepan. Add the salt and stir to dissolve. Ladle the hot brine over the okra, covering the okra by ½ inch and leaving an additional ½ inch of headspace between the top of the liquid and the top of the jar. Use a bubble tool, or other nonmetallic implement, to release any trapped air.

PRESERVE

3. Use the boiling-water method (see page 95). Wipe the rims, cover the jars, and screw the bands on just fingertip-tight. Process for 15 minutes. Cool for 24 hours. Check the seals and store in a cool, dark place for up to 1 year.

Q I have seen some websites that say vegetables in water can be processed with the boiling-water method if they are processed for 2 to 3 hours.

A It is never safe to process un-acidified vegetables using the boiling-water method. Without acid, the boiling point is just not high enough to destroy any lingering bacteria that can lead to contamination. *Always pressure can vegetables in water and process them for the amount of time indicated in your recipe.*

Filling the Jars

Q When should I use the cold-pack method?

A The cold-pack method simply means packing raw food into your canning jars. Typically the food is then covered with a hot liquid, such as a pickling brine or syrup, before processing. Cold packing is the method of choice for fragile fruits, such as peeled tomatoes, that would fall apart if heated before packing. Cold packing also makes it easier to organize produce neatly in the jar. So if you want your asparagus spears and carrots to stand up nice and tall, cold packing is the way to go (see page 81 for more on cold versus hot packing). The recipe for pickled okra on page 110 uses the cold-pack method, which allows the lovely pods to be arranged nicely in the jar.

Q Can I hot pack dill spears?

A Hot packing can be difficult for foods that will soften during the cooking process, making them hard to organize in the jar. Asparagus spears, carrot sticks, green beans, and cucumber spears need the rigidity of their raw textures to get a good pack. Save hot packing for pourable recipes that can be loaded in with a funnel (see page 81 for more on cold versus hot packing).

Loading the Canner

Q Do I load my jars into the canner as I put the lids on or wait until they are all lidded and then submerge them all at once?

A It's best to fill, bubble, clean, and lid all of your jars and then put them all into the canner at once. If you are working alone, completing each step for all of the jars before moving on to the next step is most efficient. So it's fill all, bubble all, clean all, lid all, and put all in the canner. By applying each step of the process to the whole batch rather than going through the whole process one jar at a time, you will save time and minimize your risk of skipping a step. After a few cases of tomatoes, all of the jars start to look alike, and it's hard to remember which got its bubbles removed and which is waiting for a lid cleaning.

If you are working in a group, you can set up a little assembly line where each person takes a job and you move the filled jar down the line. So one person fills and passes to the person bubbling, then that person passes it to the cleaner, and then it's passed on to someone else to apply the lids.

In either case, all steps are completed for all jars before they are placed in the hot water of the canner. Loading the canner all at once ensures that all of your jars are in the hot water for the same amount of time — so you won't be processing some more than others.

Q My pot isn't big enough to hold my jars upright. Can I can them on their sides?

A Your jars must always be lowered into the canner in their upright position and removed in the same manner. Even tipping the jars going into or out of the canner can cause the contents to leak and prevent a good seal. It can be tempting to tip the little pool of accumulated water off of the top of the jars as you are lifting them out of the canner, but you shouldn't do it, because you risk losing some of the contents of the jar.

It's hard to think of it, but the lids aren't really *on* your jars. They are just being held in place, lightly, by the ring that you have screwed on fingertip-tight. The jars haven't sealed until after they have been processed and allowed to cool for 24 hours. Up until that point, it is imperative that they remain perfectly upright, before and during processing and during the 24-hour cooldown period, to ensure a tight seal.

For the best results, always can in a pot that is at least 3 inches taller than the tallest jar you will be using. This height allows for the jars to remain upright and for hot water to circulate all around, including under the rack, with 2 inches of water over the jars, too.

It is also important to load a full layer of jars into the canner, even if you are using only a few, so that the filled jars won't tip over during processing.

The canner must be 3" taller than the tallest jar

Q Can I load my filled jars into cold water and then bring it to a boil?

A When you use the boiling-water method, you want to load your filled jars into a canner full of hot water. This is important for a number of reasons. You don't want to load hot jars full of hot liquid into cold water; the temperature change can stress the glass and cause it to crack. You also don't want to cool your hot food, which would throw off your processing time. Submerging your hot filled jars in cold water can also allow the unsealed jars to seep, disrupting the amount of headspace and ultimately the chance of getting a good seal.

It's important to always have your canner ready and waiting for your filled jars. Turn on the heat and bring it to a boil while you prepare your recipe. If it comes to a boil sooner than you need it, keep the lid on and turn off the heat. Then you can just turn the heat back on when you are ready to proceed.

Q Can I process different recipes at the same time?

A The simple answer is, yes, you can process different recipes at the same time, *but* you have to do a little advance planning.

Of course, the easiest scenario is when you have two recipes that process for the same amount of time. The only trick then is to make sure that they finish their cooking at roughly the same time, so they can be jarred up and are ready for the canner before cooling off. (You never want your filled jars to cool before being loaded into the canner or else they will be underprocessed.) It might sound hard, but it's really not if you choose compatible recipes. At least one of them has to be a low-maintenance recipe, like a sauce that is just cooking down and needs an occasional stir. That way, you can devote more than half of your attention to the higher-maintenance creation, say, a jam that needs to be tested for gel. Trying to get two batches of jam to gel at the same time without scorching them sounds like a recipe for disaster, or at least no fun, so I don't recommend it. Once you have your recipes done, fill your jars, then load everything into the canner at once, and process as directed.

If you want to process jars that have different processing times, it can be done, but it is a bit trickier. You have to get your pacing down just right. But it is possible to load in several jars that need to be processed longer, then load in another batch that will be processed for a fraction of the first batch's processing time. Be careful that you do not lose the boil while loading in the second batch. Having a large canner where the ratio of water to jars is very high will help this, as will loading in smaller jars in the second batch. Here's an example of how it would look:

0:00   Load filled pints of chutney into the canner for 20 minutes processing.

10:00   Load filled 8-ounce jars of jam into the canner for 10 minutes processing.

20:00   Turn the canner off, and remove the lid.

25:00   Remove all the jars from the canner.

Processing

Q When does processing time start?

A Processing time starts after you have placed all of your filled jars in your canner and it comes to a full, rolling boil. That means that big bubbles are rising and popping with gusto on the top of the water, almost threatening to erupt out of the pot.

boiling, circulating water

Once this boiling begins, you can start your timer. You can reduce the heat a bit if a boilover looms, but you should maintain a good active boil, not a simmer. It is also imperative that you maintain at least 2 inches of boiling water over the top of the lids, so if your water starts to evaporate below that point, top it off with a little extra boiling water from a kettle or small pan kept at the ready.

Q How does altitude affect processing time?

A Water boils at 212°F at sea level. Decreased air pressure at higher elevations lowers the boiling point. To compensate, processing time must be increased so that the food in the jars is heated through properly. If you are canning at an increased elevation, use the following chart to adjust your processing times (and enjoy the view!).

Elevation	Increase in Processing Time
1,001 to 3,000 feet	5 minutes
3,001 to 6,000 feet	10 minutes
Over 6,000 feet	15 minutes

Q My filled jars are bobbing in my canner. How can I keep them submerged?

A Bobbing jars are a sign that something is wrong. Only empty or partially empty jars would float. Either they have not been filled properly or they have lost a good bit of their contents during processing. Properly filled jars will stay submerged.

Q Can I process my jars in the dishwasher?

A Processing your jars in boiling water or a pressure canner is the only way to guarantee safe and consistent results. The water and steam surround the jars thoroughly, allowing the heat to penetrate completely. Processing them in the dishwasher, oven, or by any other heat source may not allow the heat to circulate completely and is not recommended.

Q I got called away from the kitchen after I prepared my bread-and-butter pickles. Can I just reheat them before I process them?

A It's important when you are canning to move through the process without delay. That's not to say that you have to work in some sort of white-knuckled panic, but the delay of a trip to the store for more jars, or of 20 minutes spent scrounging around for your tongs, is not going to give you the best result. Before you start, it's important to have all of your equipment organized, washed, and laid out so that everything is at your fingertips. You can whistle while you work, chat on the phone, crank up the tunes, or invite your friends into the kitchen for company, but you shouldn't stop and start. Never refrigerate your cooked recipe and process it the following day. Significant pauses in your project can allow bacteria to proliferate, produce to soften, and sweet spreads to overcook and go tarry.

Q What should I do if the water boils down below the tops of my jars during processing?

A For safe and consistent results, jars need to be completely surrounded by boiling water during processing. This means that they need to be elevated on a canning rack and submerged under at least 2 inches of boiling water for the duration of the processing time indicated in the recipe.

If your jars were not covered with water during processing, they may not have sealed correctly or the food may not have heated through to its center, conditions that can lead to contamination and spoilage.

Keep a pot of boiling water or a preheated kettle handy during processing and top up your canner if it begins to boil down. If the water boils down below the tops of the jars during processing, add enough water to cover by 2 inches, return to a boil, and restart your processing time.

Q My pot stopped boiling during processing. Can I just start my timing from where I left off?

A Unfortunately, you have to start from square one again. Processing time starts when the filled canner regains a full, rolling boil and is valid only if the canner maintains that boil throughout its duration. Any interruption will allow the food to lose temperature and will throw your timing off, resulting in underprocessed food, which is more likely to spoil. Keep your canner covered to help maintain a steady boil and monitor it during the first part of processing, adjusting as necessary to keep the boil going. Only walk away once you are confident that you have adjusted your heat appropriately.

Q Why do you let the jars rest in the hot water after processing?

A During processing, the contents of your jars heat all the way through. If you look down into your canner during processing, you can often see the contents bubbling and moving around in the jars as they process. The contents of your jars are still very hot right after processing, even if you have turned off the heat and the water is no longer at a boil. It's important to let your jars rest for 5 minutes to let them cool off just a bit so that the contents have a chance to settle back down into the jars. If you pull the jars out of the canner while it is still boiling or directly after the boil, the hot, still-active liquid in the jars can squirt out the top. At the worst, the squirting can scald you, and at the least it will ruin your seal. Always give your jars the 5-minute rest for safety and good sealing.

Q I just removed my jars from the canner and they have more headspace than when they went in. What happened?

A A few things can cause your jars to have more headspace coming out of the canner than they did going in. Here are some of the most common causes:

- Air was trapped in the jars before processing. Always swirl a nonmetallic stick, skewer, or a bubble tool around the inside of your jar to remove trapped air. Pay special attention to jars containing halved or whole fruits, as these can have some of the largest air bubbles either caught in the divots left when their pits or cores were removed or trapped in the spaces between the large pieces of fruit. In addition to bubbling them, it's a good idea to swirl them around from side to side to release air bubbles caught within or between the fruit bits.

- A small amount of food material may have been trapped between the rim of the jar and the lid during processing, allowing food to seep out. Always wipe jar rims thoroughly to ensure that they are free of any seeds, brine, or syrup that could prevent a good seal.

- The jars may have been overfilled. Food expands when heated and can push up against the lid during processing, allowing liquid to escape. Always fill jars to the proper headspace to prevent overfilling.

- Air trapped in the cell walls of your produce was released during processing, causing the contents to deflate. Always cook your food for as long as indicated in the recipe. Pack raw foods well.

- Jam or jelly was too hot when ladled into your jars. While you never want your recipe to cool before you can it, it's important to let thick mixtures such as jams and jellies rest for 5 minutes off of the heat to allow any air in them to settle out before filling your jars.

- The jars may have overprocessed. Jars that are boiled for longer than indicated can bubble out some of their contents into the canning water. Always process precisely for the time indicated in the recipe.

- The rings were on too loose. Always make sure that your rings are screwed down fingertip-tight to get a good seal.

Checking for a Seal

Q Why didn't my jars seal?

A Every canner experiences the occasional seal failure. A number of things can contribute to it. Sometimes it's something that's out of your hands: perhaps a little seed bubbled up under the lid during processing and got lodged between the lid and the jar. Other times, the seal failure could have been prevented. Here are some of the most common causes of seal failure and the best way to steer clear of them:

- **Chipped rim.** Any nick or chip in the rim of your jar will prevent a good seal. Always check used jars to make sure they are in good shape by running your finger around the rim before loading them into your canner.

- **Food particles.** Any lingering material on the rim of the jar — food, brine, syrup, seeds, and spices — can interfere with a good seal. Be sure to clean the rims of your jar carefully to ensure good results.

- **Used or hard gaskets.** Trying to reuse single-use lids or using lids or gaskets that are old can lead to seal failure. Always use a fresh lid for canning. Single-use lids should not be more than 5 years old or the gasket may be too dry to seal. Always make sure reusable gaskets are flexible, not dry or cracked.

- **Overpacked jars.** If your jars are too full, the contents can push up on the lid during processing and prevent a good seal. Always fill to the amount of headspace indicated. Be particularly careful with foods that expand during processing, such as corn.

Q I see traces of salsa in the water in my canner. Is this okay?

A *Traces?* Yes, that's okay. Salsa soup? Not a good sign. It's not uncommon for a tiny bit of a jar's contents to escape during processing. After all, it is the venting of gases from inside the jar to the outside that creates the vacuum seal. Sometimes that venting carries with it a few drops of salsa or jam or pickling liquid, and that's okay. Just be sure to check the seals after cooling to make sure that a little seed or fruit matter hasn't prevented an airtight fit between the jar rim and lid.

However, a significant amount of food in the canner means that something has gone wrong. It may be that the lids were not positioned on top of the jars, the jars were not sealed fingertip-tight, or the jars were filled beyond the recommended headspace and the pressure of the expanding food kept the lid from sealing down on the food. Inspect your jars. Even if the jars have sealed, if there is excessive headspace, you need to refill and reprocess your jars for safe storage.

Q When I tipped the water off the top of my processed jars, some of the contents leaked out. Can I just clean them up and let them seal?

A Leaking contents will almost certainly affect the headspace and can very well lodge some debris between the lid and rim of the jar. Not a good recipe for safe storage. Better to store them in the fridge and enjoy them within 3 weeks.

It's always best to use canning tongs to lift jars straight up and out of the water after processing. While it's tempting to tip the little lake of water off the top of the jar, don't do it! Just let that little pool evaporate as your jars rest and cool.

Q One of my jars didn't seal. Is the food safe to eat?

A Even the most experienced canner will occasionally have a jar that just doesn't seal. Maybe it was slightly overfilled, the lid wasn't cleaned completely, or a little seed got trapped under the rim during processing. While an unsealed jar is not shelf stable, its contents don't have to be thrown away. Just store that jar in the refrigerator and enjoy within 3 weeks.

CHAPTER 6

Pressure Canning

If you want to can nonacidic foods, you need to break out your pressure canner. Nonacidic items would be vegetables without added acids, and meat, fish, and tofu, and any recipe containing vegetables without added acids, or meat, fish, or tofu. It is not a difficult process, but it requires a pressure canner (not a pressure cooker!) to do it. Read on and find out more about pressure canning.

Basics

Q Why pressure can?

A Pressure canning is essential for the safe processing of nonacidic recipes. Such recipes include any vegetables without added acid, as well as meat, fish, or tofu or any recipe that contains meat, fish, or tofu. These items *cannot* be canned with the boiling-water method. I cannot stress it enough: Nonacidic recipes *must* be pressure canned.

Pressure canning processes food at a higher temperature than the boiling-water method. In the boiling-water method, jars are submerged in boiling water, which reaches a temperature of 212°F at sea level. Pressure canning uses a specialized canner that locks the lid in place. This sealing mechanism creates a pressurized environment that raises the processing temperature above the boiling point. The higher temperature destroys pathogens that would survive at the boiling point, and this temperature difference allows nonacidic foods to be preserved safely.

It is critical that you use only approved recipes designed for the canning method you will be using and that you adhere to these recipes completely. Using the boiling-water method to process nonacidic recipes is a grave mistake, one that can easily lead to contamination.

While you don't need to know the specific pH of the recipes you will be canning, it's helpful to know the difference between what an acidic and a nonacidic recipe looks like. Here is a short, though by no means exhaustive, list of the kinds of recipes that would fall into each of these two categories, just to give you a sense of the dividing line. Always follow your recipe and use the processing method indicated.

Boiling-Water Method (Acidic)
- Corn relish
- Tomato sauce
- Fruit juice
- Whole fruit
- Pickled carrots
- Pepper relish
- Tomato-based barbecue sauce
- Tomato-based cocktail sauce
- Tomato salsa

Pressure Can (Nonacidic)
- Shucked corn
- Tomato sauce with meat
- Chicken stock
- Whole vegetables
- Carrots in water
- Chili con carne
- Chicken meat
- Seafood
- Vegetable soup

Q I want to pressure can but I am afraid the thing is going to explode.

A The exploding canner is an image that looms large in the minds of many who have considered giving the process a try. And, until relatively recently, exploding canners were a very real possibility. They were heavy-walled cauldrons that were cumbersome and not always the easiest to operate. Modern pressure canners, those manufactured since the 1970s, however, are thinner-walled designs with built-in safety features that prevent the "tomato bombs" of canners past. Today, canners come with pressure release valves — gaskets that will release excess steam if the pressure gets too high. No more tomatoes on the ceiling. Promise.

Q How does a pressure canner work?

A Pressure canners are tightly covered pots that trap steam inside them to build up air pressure and, therefore, raise the processing temperature above the boiling point. This higher temperature allows you to process foods such as meat, fish, and un-acidified vegetables, which would not be heated effectively at the lower temperature of boiling water.

Q What's the difference between a dial-gauge canner and a weighted-gauge canner?

A **The weighted-gauge canner** is self-regulating. It uses a weighted disk over the vent pipe to control the pressure inside the canner. The weight is divided into 5-pound increments, with 5-, 10-, 15-, and 20-pound notches. You can use only these selections to designate the pressure.

The dial-gauge canner is controlled by regulating the intensity of the heat source. You must manually adjust the cooking temperature until the proper pressure is reached. You must also monitor the canner during processing to ensure that the correct pressure is being maintained by adjusting the heat accordingly. Processing times for dial-gauge pressure canners often indicate very fine gradations of increased pressure to correspond with increased altitude.

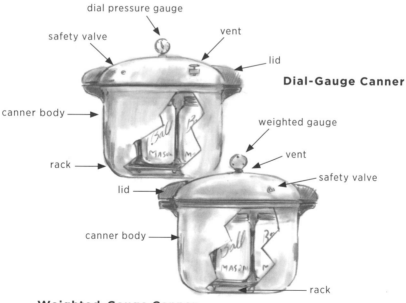

dial pressure gauge

safety valve

vent

lid

Dial-Gauge Canner

canner body

weighted gauge

vent

rack

safety valve

lid

canner body

rack

Weighted-Gauge Canner

Q My friend got burned by the steam in her pressure canner. How do you keep that from happening?

A Most likely, your friend opened the canner before it was completely cooled. You must allow your canner to return to zero pressure before opening it. Make sure to remove your gauge to allow excess steam to escape before removing the lid. Even then, it's always advisable to tip the lid away from you to avoid any steam from being released toward your face or body. Never force-cool a pressure canner by pouring cold water over it or wrapping it with cold towels.

Q What does it mean to exhaust or vent your canner? Why is it important?

A *Exhausting* your canner, also called *venting*, allows the pressure in your canner to become constant before you begin to measure and regulate it. It's a simple part of the pressure-canning process that ensures your readings are accurate. After the lid is closed on your filled canner and it is placed over a burner, steam will begin to build and escape through the vent pipe. This will start slowly at first but in a few minutes, the steam will form a distinct cone shape as it is released through the vent pipe. Once the cone has formed, regulate the heat to maintain a steady, robust flow of steam for 10 minutes, exhausting the canner. After this step, you can put your weighted or dial gauge in place to reach the appropriate pressure.

Q If I double the number of jars that I am processing, do I double the amount of time they are in the canner?

A No. Processing times are determined by the recipe and the size of the canning jar. The number of jars in the canner, even if you are processing double layers of jars, is irrelevant.

Q I'm in a hurry. Can't I just submerge my pressure canner in some cold water to cool it down quickly?

A It is crucial that you allow your pressure canner to return to zero pressure gradually and naturally. Never submerge it in water or apply cold towels to hasten the process. Doing so can damage your pressure canner and cause the jars inside to leak their contents or crack.

Q What are the basic steps to pressure canning?

A Pressure canning and the boiling-water method share a lot of the same steps. The difference lies in how you process the jars. Rather than submerging the jars in boiling water, as you would with the boiling-water method, pressure-canned jars are subjected to a highly pressurized environment that raises the temperature above the boiling point. If you have ever used the boiling-water method to process food, you will find pressure canning an easy leap to make. Even if you've never canned food before, pressure canning is pretty straightforward. Here's how it goes:

1. **Wash your equipment and jars.** You don't need to use any special cleansers, but it's important that all of your equipment be clean. Wash everything in hot, soapy water and arrange on a clean tea towel. Separate your jars into their three components, wash them in hot, soapy water, and set aside.

2. **Prepare your canner.** Wash your canner and rack and set it on a burner. Inspect all of your dials, gauges, and seals to ensure that they are in good working order. Vents should be clear; any gaskets should be flexible, with no cracks or dryness. Add cold water to your canner to the fill level indicated.

3. **Prepare your recipe.** Now that everything is clean and arranged, it's time to make your recipe. If you are pressure canning raw foods, pack your jars. Using a canning funnel or a small ladle to prevent spills, gently fill the jars to the headspace recommended in your recipe. Use a bubble tool or other nonmetallic instrument to swipe the insides of the jar to release any trapped air. Wipe the rims with a damp paper towel. Center the lids on the jars. Screw the bands on just fingertip-tight.

4. **Vent the canner.** Load the jars into the pressure canner (A). Place and seal the lid. With the vent fully open, begin to heat your pressure canner. When a cone of steam is exuberantly emitting, start timing. Allow the steam to continue to escape for 10 minutes to vent the canner (B).

5. **Achieve pressure.** Insert the weighted or dial gauge. To achieve pressure with a weighted gauge, use the guidelines provided with the unit to select the desired psi and insert the gauge. The weighted gauge will "burp" or rock occasionally to release steam and maintain pressure. To reach pressure with a dial gauge, adjust the heat until the desired pressure is reached. Continue to check the pressure to ensure accuracy. Process for the time indicated in the recipe (C).

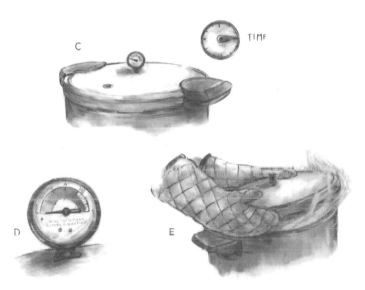

6. **Cool the canner.** Once processing is complete, turn off the burner and allow the canner to cool naturally. Do not submerge it in cold water or wrap with cold towels to hasten the process. When the pressure reaches zero (D), remove the gauge to allow excess steam to escape. Unlock the lid and tip it away from you, allowing any residual steam to escape (E).

7. **Remove the jars.** Using canning tongs, remove the jars from the canner and transfer to a towel-covered surface. Allow to cool for 24 hours. Check the seals. Sealed jars may be stored in a cool, dry place for up to 1 year.

Q Do I need to cover my jars with water when using a pressure canner?

A No, the jars do not need to be submerged in water in the pressure canner. In fact, you need space in the canner for steam to build and create the increased pressure that allows you to safely can nonacidic recipes. Most pressure-canning recipes call for 2 to 3 inches of water on the bottom of the canner before you load it with jars, which amounts to no more than 2 to 3 quarts, depending on the size of your canner. Always check the manufacturer's instructions for the precise water level for your pressure canner.

Q Can I stack my jars in my pressure canner?

A Yes, you can stack up to two layers of jars in your pressure canner, as long as it is tall enough to accommodate this layering. Be sure to use a canning rack between layers to keep the jars from resting directly on top of each other, and for best results, stagger your jars so that the ones on top aren't lined up directly above the ones on the bottom.

Q Do I need to sterilize my equipment?

A Recipes that are processed in a pressure canner, just like those that will be processed using the boiling-water method for more than 10 minutes, do not require presterilization of your equipment or jars. The high temperatures of the process will eradicate any potential contaminants.

Q Should I hot pack or cold pack when pressure canning?

A You can use either the hot-pack or the cold-pack method for pressure canning. Even meats can be packed raw or cooked in stews, chilies, or hash and then pressure canned. Follow processing times for the kind of pack used to fill the jars.

Q Can I use my pressure canner outside?

A Using a pressure canner outside is not advisable. Keeping a constant pressure in the canner is critical to success. Any passing breeze may disrupt the flame and cause you to lose pressure. Additionally, the high temperatures of outdoor cookers can warp or damage the bottom of a pressure canner, ruining the equipment.

Q My jars always come out of the pressure canner with a whitish coating on the outside. Is this okay?

A That whitish film is just a water stain. You can avoid it by adding a little white vinegar (2 teaspoons per 1 quart) to the water in your pressure canner. After they have completely cooled, make sure to wipe down your jars thoroughly before storing them — you may even consider giving them a quick rinse. Any vinegar residue could corrode the lid, leading to rust. Wash your canner thoroughly before storage to prevent any vinegar residue from pitting the inside of your pressure canner.

Equipment

Q What kind of jars should I use with a pressure canner?

A You always need to use canning jars in the pressure canner. Their extra-thick glass is essential for the increased pressure of the process. Recycled jars from store-bought products — even if they look like canning jars — are likely to shatter and are not recommended for any kind of canning.

Standard, three-piece jars are most commonly used for both the boiling-water method and for pressure canning, and they give a reliable result. Clamp-type jars with removable seals can also be used (you need to use more clamps to hold the lids in place) but are reported to have increased seal failure when used with pressure canning.

Q I got a pressure cooker for Christmas. Can I use that to pressure can?

A Well, that depends. Some pressure canners can be used as pressure cookers, but not all pressure cookers can be used as pressure canners. Pressure cookers that are designed just for whipping up batches of beans, roasts, and risottos will turn out your dinner quickly and easily but aren't large enough to accommodate canning jars. The USDA recommends that any pressure canner used for preserving food be large enough to hold at least 4 quart-size canning jars for safe and consistent results. Additionally, some pressure canners have instructions advising against cooking foods such as beans and rice in them because the food starches can clog the sensitive pressure gauges on these units. Always check the manufacturer's instructions for a complete list of foods that are appropriate to prepare with your canner/cooker.

Q Can I use a pressure canner as a water-bath canner?

A Yes, you can use your pressure canner as a water-bath canner. Just use the lid as you would a normal pot lid, without clamping it down onto the pot. It's the clamped lid that allows steam, and therefore pressure, to build up. If you don't seal your pressure canner, it will act just like a normal pot with a lid.

One thing to keep in mind, however, is that pressure canners can be very heavy, particularly those with thick-sided walls. So you may want to place it on your burner and then use a pitcher to transfer water from the spigot to the canner to fill it rather than trying to move the canner full of water and jars onto the stove.

Q What kind of maintenance does a pressure canner need?

A Pressure canners have some precision elements that indicate and regulate pressure. It's important that these features be inspected regularly to ensure that they are in proper working order. Gaskets must be clean and pliable, and vent pipes and air vents should be clear of any material that might clog them.

The pressure dial gauge on a weighted-gauge canner is used for informational purposes only — to let you know when the canner has completely cooled, for example — and is nonessential to the functioning of the canner.

The dial on a dial-gauge canner, however, is used to help regulate the pressure, so it must be in perfect working order to guarantee safe results. Have your dial gauge checked by your local ag extension at least once per season and replace if inaccurate.

Q The pressure in my canner shot up suddenly into the danger zone. What happened?

A A few things can happen to cause the pressure in your canner to rise dramatically. Most likely, there was a clog in the venting mechanism. It's imperative that all gaskets, valves, and parts be clean and in good working order. Food particles and oils can gum up these essential elements and prevent steam from escaping, causing your pressure to increase rapidly. You may also have your heat source too high. It's important, particularly with a dial-gauge canner, to diligently monitor the heat source so that you can maintain accurate pressure.

Q The inside of my pressure canner is getting discolored. What can I do?

A You can prevent discoloration by adding a couple of tablespoons of distilled white vinegar to the water during processing. Be sure to wash your sealed and cooled jars thoroughly to remove any traces of the vinegar from the lids; otherwise the acid might corrode the metal and loosen the seal. An occasional polishing with a cleaner designed specifically for aluminum can also restore the luster to older canners.

What to Pressure Can

Q I put meat in my tomato sauce, so which method should I use to preserve it?

A Any recipe that contains meat, fish, or un-acidified vegetables must be processed in a pressure canner. Doing so raises the temperature to a safe point that cannot be reached using the boiling-water method.

Q Can I pressure can my leftovers?

A Your instinct to save is to be commended. Better to freeze leftovers than can them, however. The small amounts would make a lot of work for a little food. And without a proven recipe, it's impossible to recommend correct processing times and pressures.

Q Can I pressure can my jams and salsas to save time?

A Jams and salsas are acidic, so they can be canned using the boiling-water method. The high heat of pressure canning can overprocess these items, causing the pectin to separate out and the final product to have a soft, unpleasant texture. By the time the pressure canner is vented, the food is processed, and the canner is allowed to cool down, you won't be saving any time by pressure canning these items. Use the boiling-water method instead.

Q Can I can vegetables in water?

A Yes, but you have to use a pressure canner to do it. Vegetables without any added acid do not have a pH low enough to can with the boiling-water method.

Q Can I pressure can actual cans of food?

A Yes, you can use a pressure canner to process food sealed in cans. However, the process is not as common as canning in jars. You need to purchase a can sealer and the cans.

Q Can I can bread?

A Bread is not suitable for canning. If you want to give such a gift, consider blending all of the dry ingredients for a bread or cake mix in a canning jar along with instructions for adding the fresh, wet ingredients and baking. Some mixes, such as those for recipes with chocolate morsels and other textured items, can be layered decoratively in the jar, sort of like sand art. It's cute (and safe!).

Q I have this awesome recipe for black bean salsa. Can I can it?

A Even though pressure canning is meant for canning nonacidic recipes, not all nonacidic recipes are appropriate for the method. Most of the recipes approved for pressure canning are very simple, single-ingredient or single types of ingredient (such as mixed vegetables) formulas that are meant to be used as building blocks for great cooking, not eaten directly out of the jar. Best to can your vegetable salsa and beans separately and then combine them before serving.

GREEN BEANS IN WATER

Adapted from the USDA recipe

Instructions for pressure-canning recipes aren't recipes, per se. They are instructions on process. You can use the details below as a guide to canning all vegetables in water, adjusting headspace, processing time, and pressure as necessary for the particular vegetable you are canning.

INGREDIENTS

1 pound beans per pint jar (2 pounds per quart jar), trimmed and left whole or cut into 1-inch pieces

½ teaspoon kosher salt per pint (optional)

PREPARE

1. You can either cold pack or hot pack your beans.

To cold pack, arrange the beans, upright, in your hot, clean jars. Add the salt, if using. Fill the jars with boiling water, leaving 1 inch of headspace.

To hot pack, boil your cut beans in water for 5 minutes. Add the salt, if using. Ladle into your jars, leaving 1 inch of headspace.

PRESERVE

2. Use the pressure-canning method (see page 126). Process both hot-pack and cold-pack pints for 20 minutes and quarts for 25 minutes at 11 psi if using a dial-gauge canner and 10 psi if using a weighted-gauge canner (adjust for altitude, if necessary). Cool for 24 hours. Check the seals and store in a cool, dark place for up to 1 year.

CHAPTER 7

Refrigeration

Refrigeration as a home food preservation method? You bet. Think of it as a root cellar that you plug into the wall. It keeps food in a cool, dark place, giving you more time to enjoy it.

I've spent time in a New Hampshire camp that still uses traditional iceboxes, cooled by ice harvested from the nearby lake in winter — not nearly as efficient as today's modern models, but charming indeed. Whether it's an icebox, a double-door, top-of-the-line giant, or even a dark cave, keeping food cool is a trusted trick for keeping it fresh.

Q **What's the difference between a refrigerator pickle and other kinds of pickles?**

A Refrigerator pickles rely on the chill of the fridge rather than a specific level of acid to preserve them. Because you don't have to be precise about the pH level, you can experiment with your recipes more freely. For example, unlike pickles destined for the boiling-water method, which rely on the pH power of 5 percent acidity vinegar, you can use all kinds of different vinegars to flavor your refrigerator pickles.

Making fridge pickles is very simple. You make a brine of vinegar (diluted with a bit of water, if you like) and flavorings — at the least a bit of salt and sugar, but you can add anything you like. Place your prepared produce in a heatproof container, bring your brine to a boil, and pour it over the produce. Let cool to room temperature and then refrigerate.

Here are a few flavor combinations to get you started:

- Apple cider vinegar, salt, pepper, sugar, celery seeds, mustard seeds

- Red wine vinegar, salt, sugar, garlic

- Rice wine vinegar, soy sauce, fish sauce, sugar

- Distilled white vinegar, sugar, chili paste

- White wine vinegar, salt, sugar, fennel seeds

Brine Ingredients for Refrigerator Pickles

mustard seeds

vinegar

chili paste

soy sauce

head of garlic

sugar

salt

Q How long will my refrigerator pickles last in the icebox?

A That depends on the recipe. The range can be anywhere from a few days to a few weeks. Delicate ingredients, such as thinly sliced red onion, will go limp from the brine sooner than sturdier items, such as carrots and beets. The level of acidity will also affect their lifespan. Weaker brines won't protect foods as well as strong ones with plenty of vinegar. While you are free to experiment, it's a good idea to keep the vinegar content significant — at least 50 percent of the brine volume — so that you get a longer time to enjoy your pickles. Keep in mind that produce will release its water when submerged in brine, weakening it a bit, so a brine that tastes a little assertive at the outset might very well be just right after a few days of mingling in the jar.

Q Can I can recipes for refrigerator pickles?

A Refrigerator pickles are a great way to extend the shelf life of produce quickly and easily. And because the cool temperatures of the fridge keep them safe rather than the pH of their brine, they are a fun way to experiment with different flavors and strengths of vinegars that may lack the pH punch necessary for safe processing. While this flexibility is great in the fridge, it is unsafe on the shelf. Only recipes that have been tested and are known to have a pH of 4.6 or less are safe for canning. Refrigerator pickles are often much less acidic than those destined for canning and don't qualify for the process.

Q Can I just refrigerate my jam?

A Yes, refrigeration is a great alternative for time-pressed preservers. Just prepare your recipe as you normally would, cool, cover, and refrigerate. You can expect low-sugar jams and jellies (those that use less than a 1:1 proportion of sugar to fruit) to keep for about 3 weeks. So, unless you are a big jam eater, you might want to stick to small-batch recipes or gift some away so it can be enjoyed before it expires. Full-sugar jams will keep longer before they start to mold over.

Refrigerating marmalades, however, is not recommended. It's not a safety issue as much as one of flavor. The marmalade needs a few weeks to ripen in the jar — for the flavors to mellow and blend — for optimum flavor. The cool temperatures and shorter storage time will limit the ability for the marmalade to reach its full flavor potential.

Q What's the best way to pickle eggs?

A Refrigerator pickling is the only method recommended for curing hard-boiled eggs. If you are like me, you might remember a jug of pickled eggs lingering on the elbow of a well-worn bar, left open and available for anyone who needed a little snack. A nice image, but maybe not the safest practice — for safety's sake,

keep your eggs refrigerated at all times. A few more tips for safe, tasty results:

- Make sure your eggs are fully cooked, with hard yolks. This is not a good recipe for soft-cooked eggs.
- Be sure that your eggs are fully submerged in your brine. Eggs exposed to air will spoil quickly.
- You can reuse the brine from pickled beets or other pickles to pickle your eggs. Combine the brine 1:1 with fresh vinegar (and additional spices if you like) and bring it to a boil before pouring over your eggs.
- Season your eggs by allowing them to steep in the brine for 2 to 3 weeks before enjoying them.
- Pickled eggs, completely submerged in brine, will keep in the refrigerator for 3 to 4 months

Q Can I pickle food that has been in my root cellar?

A Food used for shelf-stable canning should be as fresh as possible for the most consistent results. Produce stored in a root cellar often loses its moisture content during its time in storage and can give you less-than-perfect results.

I do, however, love to make refrigerator pickles out of my root cellar vegetables. Their tang is a great alternative to salads in the months when greens are less available. And for root cellar products that are starting to fade in quality, it's a great way to squeeze a little extra time and flavor out of them. Because refrigerator pickles rely on the cool temperatures of the icebox rather than proper pH to stay wholesome, you have much more latitude for experimentation. Feel free to make substitutions, adjusting these ideas to your tastes. You can scale the recipes up or down to suit the amount of produce you have on hand, just be sure to make enough to keep your produce fully submerged during storage. On the next page are two recipes to get you started.

SIMPLE BRINE

Makes 1½ cups

This simple brine is a blank canvas for any refrigerator pickle. You can use it with sliced cucumbers and red onions, radishes, turnips or kohlrabi, carrots, zucchini or summer squash cut into coins, or chiles halved or cut into rings. You can also spice up the brine with chili flakes, whole cloves or allspice, cumin, or coriander.

INGREDIENTS

1 cup red wine vinegar

½ cup water

1 tablespoon sugar

1 teaspoon salt

PREPARE

Combine the vinegar, water, sugar, and salt in a small saucepan and bring to a boil, stirring to dissolve the sugar and salt. Pour the mixture over your produce to cover and refrigerate for at least several hours and up to 3 weeks.

PUB PICKLES

Makes 1¼ cups

The malt vinegar in this brine gives it a distinctive flavor that stands up well to heartier vegetables. It's a great match for turnips and carrots, but you could also use cauliflower florets or chunks of onion. Customize the brine with flavorings such as celery, mustard, fennel, or dill seeds.

INGREDIENTS

- 1 cup white wine vinegar
- ¼ cup malt vinegar
- 1 tablespoon sugar
- 1 teaspoon salt
- ½ teaspoon black peppercorns
- chopped vegetables

PREPARE

Combine the white wine vinegar, malt vinegar, sugar, salt, and peppercorns in a small saucepan and bring to a boil, stirring to dissolve the sugar and salt. Pour the mixture over your produce to cover, and refrigerate. Marinate vegetables in the brine for at least 3 days for best flavor. Keeps, refrigerated, for up to 3 weeks.

CHAPTER 8

Freezing

Freezing is a great quick fix for preserving foods. Most everyone has a freezer and can designate a section of it for saving seasonal ingredients. If you are really into creating your own frozen food section, you can purchase a separate unit just for food saving and have locally grown foods at your fingertips all year round. Read on to find out how you can have frozen foods that taste their best.

Q Why do my frozen fruits turn brown?

A Freezing slows but does not halt the deterioration of produce. How you treat your produce before you add it to the freezer will greatly alter your results. Fruits, which tend to discolor, should be treated with an acid bath prior to freezing. To make an acid bath, dissolve ½ teaspoon or 3 crushed 500 mg tablets of ascorbic acid (vitamin C) in 1 quart of water. Soak the fruit in the solution for a few minutes, drain, and proceed with your recipe.

Kitchen Tip

Keep your freezer organized by sectioning off areas for different kinds of foods — meats, produce, baked goods, and ingredient items such as flours, meals, and stocks should all have their own designated spots. It will keep you from digging through icy cold packages and makes it easier to rotate out older items.

Q Can I freeze my canning jars?

A Yes, you can freeze canning jars. Just be sure that you leave enough room for the food to expand as it freezes or it will cleave the lid off of the jar or, worse, shatter it. I leave about 1 inch of space for pints and 2 inches for quarts.

If you want a little insurance against breakage, you can always freeze your jars without their lids. That way, food can expand above the rim if necessary, eliminating the risk of the glass breaking. After the contents are completely frozen, and no more than 48 hours later or you risk freezer burn, you can inspect your items, make sure that the contents are below the rim, and then screw the lids on.

Q What's the best way to thaw my food?

A Frozen food has the best texture when thawed slowly, allowing the ice crystals to gradually diminish in size. Quick thawing encourages the large crystals to cut the food fibers as they thaw, leading to a mushy end product.

The best and safest way to thaw is in the refrigerator. Place your frozen foods in a baking pan to catch any drips and allow them to come slowly to fridge temperature. For large cuts of meat, this can take a long time, so you'll need to plan ahead. Large cuts and whole birds can take up to 2 days. Give it time — trying to cook a partially frozen cut can easily lead to a roast or bird that is overdone outside and still raw in the center.

In a hurry? You can thaw your foods in cold running water. Seal them in a ziplock bag, press out the air, and submerge it in a pot large enough to hold the food and a good amount of cold water. Let the tap drizzle, very slowly, into the pot to continually refresh the water. As this method wastes a lot of clean water, it's best saved for small cuts and true dinner emergencies.

Another thawing trick is to place your frozen food on a thick, heavy metal surface, such as a cast-iron skillet or griddle, or in a large, heavy skillet. The metal draws out the cold very quickly — you can thaw small packages of food in a fraction of the time.

It is strongly advised to never thaw foods at room temperature. Doing so can allow the exterior of the food to come to dangerously high temperatures even when the core of the food is still frozen.

When possible, freeze foods in small amounts for quick thawing. Shape burger patties before freezing or at least freeze the ground meat in flat packages rather than thick, football shapes. Freeze cuts individually or in single layers rather than stacking them into bundles. Freeze berries, small vegetables, and cut produce individually before transferring to packaging for long-term storage.

Q What's the best way to freeze berries?

A Frozen berries are a great way to enjoy summer fruit in the winter. You can walk right by those anemic midwinter berries, secure in the knowledge that your stash of local gems will taste better than any imported imposters on display at the grocery.

Berries frozen using this method stay separate and free-flowing, so you can pour out as few or as many as you like at a time. To freeze your berries, wash, stem, and hull the berries as necessary. Dry thoroughly by gently rolling them on a few paper towels or a clean tea towel. Arrange them in a single layer on one or more baking sheets, being careful not to crowd the pan. Lay sheets flat in the freezer (you can stack several sheets on top of each other by placing "pillars" of 4-ounce canning jars at each corner of the bottom sheet). Freeze until solid, at least 4 hours and up to 2 days. Transfer the berries to a ziplock bag or other container. They will keep for up to 6 months.

Q Can I freeze cantaloupe?

A You can't freeze melon, but you can freeze melon flavor. The same high water content that turns frozen melon to mush is the trick — separated from the pulp of the fruit, this melon-flavored liquid freezes beautifully and is great to have on hand for both nonalcoholic and adult beverages. You'll be shocked at how much liquid is in a melon; you get a great yield of juice for each fruit. If you have a juicer, that's great. But if you don't, use this quick method for getting the most from your melon:

1. Cut away the rind from the melon. Remove the seeds from melons such as cantaloupe.

2. Cut the flesh into chunks.

3. Purée in a food processor or blender, working in batches as necessary.

4. Transfer the purée to a fine-mesh sieve or cheesecloth-lined colander set over a bowl.

5. Transfer the drained juice to freezer-proof containers and discard the pulp.

Q What are the best containers to use in the freezer?

A I use a variety of containers for freezing. When I can, I like to use canning jars. They are reusable, and I certainly have enough of them around. Just make sure that you leave enough space for the freezing food to expand so that you don't compromise the glass: about ½ inch for 8-ounce jars, 1 inch for pints, and 2 inches for quarts. When I first started freezing in jars, I would fill and freeze them without their lids, then screw on the tops when the food was fully frozen. That way I was sure that they had all of the expansion room they needed. Now that I trust that they won't break, I don't take this extra step, but you can if you are leery.

For larger quantities of food that won't fit into jars, I use plastic bags. They are also handy when I want to freeze items such as whole berries, because they let you press out all of the excess air around the fruit. I try to rinse and reuse when it's practical, to cut down on waste. For items that don't threaten to leak, such as bread crumbs, I often reuse bread bags from the sliced bread that I buy. I try not to use a lot of plastic in my life, so I find the "reduce, reuse, recycle" mantra keeps the amount that I do need to a pretty good minimum.

Q How can I save space in the freezer?

A Keep in mind that while an empty freezer is not an efficient one, an overstuffed freezer is not a good idea either. You want the frozen foods to have a good circulation of cold air all around them.

That being said, I have found a few tricks for better managing my space so that I can keep my freezer organized and find things more easily. One trick is to lay your freezer bags flat until they are frozen solid. If I load up a bag with chili, for example, I don't just set it in the freezer to form a squat block. I lay it flat, either on the freezer floor or, more often, in a freezer-proof tray, such as a Pyrex dish, until it is rock solid. Once frozen, you can stand such packages upright and, like file folders, thumb through them to find what you need at a glance.

Another pointer, particularly for deep chest freezers, is to organize your packages of frozen food in shallow plastic bins. Put vegetables in one, prepared foods in another, and doughs and breads and meats in their own color-coded or marked bins. Then you can lift out the top bins to quickly access the items at the bottom of the freezer rather than bulldozing through individual (and finger-freezing!) containers to find what you need.

Q What is the best way to get air out of freezer bags?

A Getting as much air as possible out of your bags is very important to maintaining the high quality of your frozen foods. Here are a few ideas:

- **Simply press out as much air as possible.** Lay your bag on the counter and smooth the unfilled part of the bag flat. Seal the bag most of the way and press again to release any trapped air. Finish sealing.

- **Use a straw.** Press out most of the air and seal the bag almost all of the way, leaving a small opening where you can insert a straw. Poke the straw in the space and suck out the remaining air. Swiftly remove the straw, sucking all the while, and seal the small opening.

- **Get a vacuum sealer.** If you do a lot of freezing, you might consider investing in a vacuum sealer. These machines extract all the air out of the bag, creating a completely airless environment for your food.

Q What is the best kind of freezer for long-term food storage?

A Chest freezers are the most efficient, so if you freeze a fair amount of food it would be your best choice. Also, if you plan on keeping a good amount of food in freezer storage, it's smart to have a separate unit designated just for this purpose to avoid the temperature shifts that your kitchen unit suffers as it gets repeatedly opened and closed during the course of a typical day.

One word of caution: If you tend to freeze a large portion of your personal meat supply — maybe you buy beef by the side, whole fish, or hunt or have friends who do — you might consider investing in a small generator. It's an added expense, but if you lose power, the backup will save your dinner and ultimately a lot of money.

Q How can I preserve green leafy vegetables such as kale?

A You have to get some of the moisture out of leafy vegetables in order for them to freeze well. One way to do that is to blanch them — plunge them into a pot of boiling water and then shock them in an ice bath; scoop them out of the cold water, squeeze out as much excess water as you can, and then wrap them up airtight for freezing. Another method is to give them a quick sauté in a little olive oil until they are bright green and tender. Let cool to room temperature and then pack them into airtight containers to freeze. Either method will give you greens that are great tossed directly into soups and stews or defrosted and added to recipes such as frittatas, pastas, and more.

Q My power has gone out. What should I do?

A Whatever you do, do *not* open the door! Your food will stay frozen solid for some time, but only if you leave the door closed for the duration of your outage. If your power is going to be out for only a few hours, your food should be fine. If the power is going to be out for longer than that, you will have to act. Some ideas:

- Plug the freezer into a generator. If you have one on hand, use it for the freezer before anything else. You are likely to have stashes of vegetables and meats that will be more costly to replace than the milk and things in your fridge. Plus, you can always keep those chilled in a cooler with ice. The freezer is the top priority.

- Transfer the food to a freezer that is working. Sounds simple enough, but it's not uncommon for the power to be out on one side of the street or just in a section of the neighborhood. Maybe a buddy can help you out.

- If you can get your hands on some dry ice, it will keep your foods frozen. Handle it carefully, as it can burn your hands instantly if handled without gloves. Put a chunk, wrapped in newspaper or cardboard, in your freezer and shut the door.

After the power comes back on, examine your food. It's important not to refreeze food that has spoiled. If you have an automatic ice machine, take a look at the cubes that were made before the storm. Have the edges softened, or have they completely melted into one big cube? If it's the former, you should be okay, but if it's the latter, chances are that your food has completely thawed. You can also open any ice cream containers and give those a gander. Has the ice cream lost its airy quality and now looks like frozen milk? That's a sign that your food has defrosted. Frozen berries that were individually frozen and are now frozen solid is also an indication that foods have completely thawed and must be discarded.

Q How long do foods keep in the freezer?

A Freezing retards decay, but it doesn't prevent it. Even items in the deep chill have a shelf life, after which they lose flavor and texture. Vegetables often benefit from a quick blanching before freezing, which deactivates enzymes that lead to degradation. All food should be wrapped well and have as much air as possible pressed out of the storage containers. The table opposite gives some rough guidelines for safe freezer storage times.

Q I've tried freezing fresh herbs, but they come out slimy when I thaw them. What's a good method for freezing herbs?

A Herbs bring terrific flavor to many dishes, so it's great to have a stash on hand. The best method I have found for keeping them in the freezer is to create herb-sicles — cubes of herbs suspended in water or oil. To make them, just purée your fresh herbs with enough oil or water to cover. Spoon the purée into the compartments of ice cube trays, cover, and freeze. Pop out a cube whenever you want a little herb flavor in your dish. The water-based herb-sicles are great in soups and stews. Oil-based pops are terrific thawed and blended into oil and vinegar or a little yogurt for a quick dip or dressing.

Food Item	Approximate Storage Time at 0°F
Fruits and Vegetables	8 to 12 months
Fish	3 to 6 months
Meat*	
Bacon	1 month
Frankfurters	2 months
Ground or stew meat	3 months
Ham	2 months
Roasts	
Beef or lamb	1 year
Pork or veal	8 months
Steak or Chops	
Beef	1 year
Lamb or veal	9 months
Pork	4 months
Variety meats	4 months
Poultry*	
Cooked, with gravy	6 months
Cooked, no gravy	1 month
Uncooked (whole) chicken or turkey	1 year
Duck or goose	6 months
Uncooked (parts) chicken	9 months
Uncooked (parts) turkey	6 months

*University of Georgia Cooperative Extension Service

CHAPTER 9

Drying

Drying food is one of the oldest forms of home food preservation. Even before there was farming, nomadic tribes would dry the food they found or caught. Today, this method of home food preservation remains a popular, low-tech process that is accessible to every home cook.

Those who dry their own food swear by it. Here are some of the best reasons to dry that I have collected along the way:

- It's an easy way to preserve small amounts of food.
- Dried food is light and compact, so it's easy to store in small spaces.
- It's economical. You don't need any specialized equipment.
- It's an easy process to master; the steps required are easy to follow.
- It's delicious and nutritious. Home-dried foods don't come with additives, preservatives, or sweeteners, making them a great addition to your diet.

Prepping

Q What are the best fruits and vegetables to dry?

A You can dry all kinds of produce, but fruit is the easiest (and most delicious in my book). The process intensifies the fruit's sweet flavor, so dried fruits pack a lot of punch. They are great eaten out of hand but are also versatile as an ingredient in both sweet and savory recipes. For example, you can reconstitute dried cherries (see recipe on page 150) in a little brandy or rum and serve them over ice cream, or use them in stuffings and salads, where their tart flavor will make your mouth water with every bite.

Q What is the best way to crack or check fruits before drying them?

A *Cracking* and *checking* are terms used interchangeably to describe the process of breaking the skin of produce so that it can dry more readily and thoroughly. It is an important step in the drying process. Foods are prepared in this way to prevent *case hardening*, a condition that occurs when items dry too quickly on the outside, creating an airtight seal that traps moisture in the food, a potential vector for contamination. Checking the produce allows internal moisture to escape so that the food dries all the way through. If your recipe calls for your produce to be checked, don't skip it.

There are a couple of different ways you can check your produce. You can do it manually, by piercing the fruit or slitting it with a sharp knife. Or you can blanch the fruit (page 40) so that the skin softens and splits. It may seem time-consuming to check all of your fruit or counterintuitive to put the food you are going to dry through such a wet process, but checking will greatly reduce the overall drying time.

Q If I am going to dry produce, does it make sense to wash it? Won't the water slow down the process?

A It's always important to wash your produce thoroughly, no matter which method you are using to preserve it. This is particularly true of drying, which will amplify the impact of any residues that remain on the food as they shrink in size. You don't need any special scrubs or washes; just run your food under plenty of cold water. Gently but thoroughly dry the produce with a tea towel or paper towel before arranging on drying racks.

Q How can I prevent my drying fruit from turning brown?

A Pretreating foods, particularly fruits that can oxidize quickly, with a dip in an acid bath can greatly reduce color loss and browning. Ascorbic acid (vitamin C), which comes in pill and powder form, is easy to come by and keep on hand for this purpose. To make an acid bath, dissolve ½ teaspoon of ascorbic acid crystals or three 500 mg ascorbic acid tablets (crush them first) in 1 quart of water. Soak the fruit in the solution for a few minutes, drain, and proceed with your recipe. Lemon juice, which contains both citric and ascorbic acid, can also be used as an anti-browning agent, though it is less effective than pure ascorbic acid.

DRIED CHERRIES

Makes about 1 cup per quart of fresh cherries

Make these dried cherries once and they will become your favorite pantry staple: substitute them for raisins in baking recipes; add them to salads for an elegant touch — try sprinkling a few over a salad of bitter greens dotted with goat cheese for a real treat. I also like to reconstitute them in a little liquor as a grown-up dessert topping: douse ½ cup of cherries with ½ cup of brandy or rum, let stand for a few hours, and then sweeten with a couple of tablespoons of honey.

INGREDIENTS

4–8 cups sweet cherries

PREPARE

1. Preheat the oven to 170°F. Line several baking sheets with tea towels and set aside. Prepare an ice-water bath in a large bowl or impeccably clean sink.

2. Bring a large pot of water to a boil. Drop the cherries into the water, no more than 1 pound at a time, and return to a boil. Blanch for 1 minute. (See Blanching, Step by Step, page 40.)

3. Scoop out the cherries with a spider or slotted spoon and plunge them into the ice-water bath. Continue blanching the cherries in batches. Remove the cherries from the ice bath with a slotted spoon and spread on the towel-covered baking sheets. Blot dry. Pit the cherries.

PRESERVE

4. Spread the pitted cherries on metal screens or cake-cooling racks set over baking sheets. Dry in the oven until the cherries are shriveled and no longer moist in the center, 5 to 7 hours. The cherries are fully dry when you can squeeze a handful and they don't stick together.

5. Let the cherries cool, and then transfer them to a covered container to *condition* for 1 week or so. Conditioning allows the dried fruit to redistribute any trapped moisture. If you notice moisture on the inside of the container, repeat the drying process for another hour. Dried cherries will keep for up to 1 year in an airtight container.

Commercially dried foods are often treated with sulfur dioxide to preserve their bright colors. While generally considered safe, sulfur dioxide can be toxic to those with sensitivity to the compound. Home food preservers rarely use sulfur to treat their produce. Untreated fruits, while not as brightly hued, are just as flavorful as their sulfured counterparts, and their subdued colors in no way indicate spoilage.

Q How do I use sulfites to pretreat my produce?

A Sulfites have been used as a pretreatment on raw and dried foods to prevent discoloration. However, many people are sensitive to sulfite compounds, causing allergic and asthmatic reactions. The FDA has banned the use of sulfites in foods that will be sold fresh to the public, such as salad bar items. Those with sensitivities should use another pretreatment, such as ascorbic acid, for foods they intend to dry.

If you choose to pretreat with sulfite, you must use U.S.P. (food-grade) or reagent-grade, not practical-grade, sodium metabisulfite. You can find suitable products where you might purchase wine-making supplies. Add 1 tablespoon to 1 quart of water to create a pretreating bath. Add your cut foods to the solution as you prepare them. Allow to soak for 10 minutes, then towel-dry and proceed with your recipe.

Q How do I keep fruit leather from sticking to the pan while drying?

A It's easy to keep fruit leather from sticking to the pan. Just be sure to line it with a sheet of parchment paper before you pour your reduced purée into the pan. The paper will keep the leather from sticking. When the leather is dry, just roll it into a log and slice right through, paper and all. The paper will act as a protective wrapper to keep the leather fresh and to keep it from sticking together during storage.

Q What are the best fruits for turning into leather?

A Most fruits make great leather. Berries, stone fruits, apples, and pears all taste great. You can mix and match, too. Combining apples

and berries, for example, helps to stretch a small amount of berries into a full batch of leather, which makes the most of the fruit's taste and your grocery budget. Even savory items such as tomatoes can make an interesting fruit leather. Just be sure to peel and pit fruit before cooking and purée until smooth to avoid any lumps in your leather, which will keep it from drying uniformly. Avoid pulpy fruits, such as bananas, which are too starchy to dry properly.

I have also combined fruits for a decorative effect. Make two batches of fruit purée, one light (from apples, peaches, or pears, for example) and one dark (from berries, for instance). Pour the light-colored purée onto your baking sheet and smooth it out. Then you can drip little dots or drizzle streaks of the darker purée onto the light purée background. Dry your patterned leather and slice as you would a single-layer fruit leather.

Q What kinds of chiles are best for drying?

A Thin-skinned varieties of chiles, such as cayenne or Thai, that allow moisture to escape are the easiest to dry. Avoid fleshy peppers such as jalapeños, which will likely rot before all of their moisture escapes.

Methods

Q Do I have to have a special dehydrator to dry my own food?

A You don't need any special equipment to dry food. You can dry it outside or in an attic that gets good air circulation. Place it on mesh racks or string foods such as chiles and beans by running a needle and thread through the stem and hanging the threaded produce in a well-ventilated area. If you live in a damp climate, you can use your oven. Set it to a low temperature. I dry at 170°F, which simultaneously dries and pasteurizes the food. Just be sure to prop the door open slightly so that the steam created by the drying fruit can escape.

Q I don't like to use the oven during the summer. Can I just dry my fruits outside in the sun?

A If you live in an arid climate, sun-drying food is an economical way to preserve large quantities of produce easily. That's why desert cultures are so rich with dried items such as dates and apricots — they would, and sometimes still do, arrange the food on mats on the roofs of the houses to dry them in the hot sun. You can do the same on screens or racks. Just make sure that they are made out of stainless steel or plastic so they don't react with the food. If you are working with items that take more than one afternoon to dry completely, such as large pieces of fruit, you might consider bringing them in overnight so that the morning dew doesn't dampen them and slow the overall process.

No matter how you dry your food, it's a good idea to give it a quick run through the oven — just 30 minutes at 160°F — to pasteurize your fully dried produce. This will kill off any pests or bacteria that may have found their way onto the produce as it dried outside.

Q Are there any dangers associated with drying food?

A You wouldn't think of drying food as being risky, but there are important things to look out for, particularly when you are drying non-acidified things such as meat and vegetables. The risk in drying these items is the same as with canning nonacidic foods: You have to take very careful steps to prevent botulism. Just as in canning, drying can create an anaerobic environment. Foods that are dried too quickly or aren't *checked* (see page 148, bottom) can become *case hardened*, in which the outside of the food essentially creates a dry, airtight shell that seals in moisture. Just as in canning, sealing nonacidic food in an airtight container can provide botulism spores with the perfect environment to reproduce and cast off their toxin, which can be deadly. To avoid any risk of contamination:

- Always follow the directions for your drying recipes carefully.

- Blanching or breaking the skin of the food (also called *checking*) is often critical to the drying process. If either of these steps is recommended, do not skip it.

- Never dry your foods at temperatures higher than those recommended. You won't speed the process and could cause the case hardening that will prevent your food from drying thoroughly enough to be safely stored on the shelf.

- Use acid baths as directed. This step not only prevents browning but also kills pathogens and lowers the pH of foods, making them easier to preserve safely.

Q What kind of screen should I dry my produce on?

A It is important that anything that comes in contact with your food be food grade. The same holds for screens. Avoid screens that have coatings or have been painted. The best screens are plain stainless steel or plastic. Be sure to wash between uses with hot, soapy water and dry thoroughly for storage.

Q What's the best way to dry herbs?

A Herbs are a very popular item to dry, and the process couldn't be easier. You can dry them in a very low oven — even the pilot light on a gas oven or the residual heat from baking will do it. You can spread them out on your counter, strewn on a rack that allows good air circulation. If you have bunches, just bundle them with a length of string and dangle them from a beam in your attic or other dry, out-of-the-way place.

You can store your herbs as they are on the stem or shake or rub the leaves off and store them in an airtight container. The latter method will preserve the flavor of the herbs better.

Q How do I know that I have removed all necessary moisture from the produce I am drying?

A It is important to make sure that your food is thoroughly but not overly dried. Food that has too much moisture will mold in its sealed container. Overdrying will compromise flavor and texture.

Most recipes will give visual cues to help you ensure that your food is properly dried. As a rule, dried fruits should be dry but pliable. You should be able to squeeze a few in your hand without them sticking together. Dried vegetables, such as dried mushrooms and green beans, will be leathery but not brittle.

To test your produce to make sure that it is properly dried, seal the dried, cooled food in an airtight container for 24 hours. If water droplets, even the tiniest mist of humidity, form on the inside of the container, your food needs a bit more drying. Repeat the drying process until the inside of the container remains dry.

Q What about vine drying?

A Vine drying is popular for dried beans (legumes, not green beans). Leave the pods on the plant until they are dry and shriveled and the beans rattle inside. Separate the beans from the pods and check for dryness by sealing them in an airtight container for 24 hours. If, after that time, there are no moisture droplets on the inside of the container, the beans are dry enough for storage. If moisture is present, the drying process must be completed either in the sun, the oven, or a dehydrator. Even beans that are dried when picked need to be treated for insect infestation. Choose one of these methods:

Freeze the beans. Load them into ziplock bags and freeze for at least 48 hours. If you will then be storing them outside of the freezer, be sure that you allow the package to come to room temperature before you open it or humidity in the air will condense on the beans and they will require additional drying.

Pasteurize the beans in the oven. Spread them in a single layer on rimmed baking sheets. Bake at 160°F for 30 minutes to kill any potentially contaminating pests. Let cool to room temperature and transfer to airtight containers for storage.

Q I am thinking of getting a dehydrator. Any pointers?

A I am not a big fan of single-use kitchen tools. But if you dry a lot of food, then buying a dehydrator might make sense for you. Raw foodists also swear by them as well, as the temperatures of the dehydrator's settings are low enough to "bake" cookies and other treats without crossing over into cooked territory. Some things to keep in mind:

- Simpler is better. Drying food is a low-tech endeavor; you don't need a lot of bells and whistles to get it done.

- Many eaters who dry their own food set their dehydrator outside so they don't heat up their kitchen. Look for one that suits your space — indoor or out.

- Think of how you will use the dehydrator. If it's only for the occasional batch of tomatoes, get the smallest one you can find. If you are looking to dry a garden, it's worth it to get one with a large capacity.

Q I candied citrus rinds and have a lot of great-tasting syrup left over. It seems a shame to pitch it.

A You are right! No need to toss that delicious syrup. You can use it to sweeten hot and cold drinks — it's great in iced tea and even better in a margarita. It's also a lovely glaze for pies and tarts. Just store it in a sealed container in the refrigerator, where it will keep for several months. Due to its high sugar content, it may crystallize in the chill of the fridge. If this happens, you can just warm it up a little by placing the jar in a pan of hot water. The crystals will melt and it will be as good as new.

Q Can I use my microwave to dry food?

A Microwaving is not a recommended method for drying foods other than herbs, which are tiny enough to perform well. All other foods would cook unevenly in this type of oven, resulting in some food that is overcooked while some remains raw. The lack of air circulation will also inhibit the process.

Storage

Q What's the best way to store dried foods?

A Dried foods should be stored in an airtight container, such as a canning jar with a lid, away from light, heat, and, of course, moisture.

It's a good idea to store your dried foods in small quantities. Each time you open the container, humidity from the air will cause some moisture reabsorption. How much depends on how humid the day. If you have a large container, your dried food will be exposed to airborne moisture many more times than it would be in a smaller container, which you might only open once or twice before you have polished off its contents.

Always inspect your dried foods before serving them. Even foods that went into the containers dry may have picked up moisture during storage. Discard any food that becomes moldy.

Q How do I keep bugs out of my dried foods?

A Pasteurization is an important step in keeping dried foods safe and free from infestation, particularly if you have dried them outside, where the environment is much less controlled than in a dehydrator or oven. It's easy to do. Just preheat your oven to 160°F, load your dried items onto a baking sheet, and bake them for 30 minutes to kill any hidden insects or bacteria that might be lingering. Remove from the oven, let cool to room temperature, and store in an airtight container. Alternatively, you can freeze your dried food in an airtight container for 2 days to destroy any pests or eggs.

Q Why aren't my dried chiles shiny like those in the store?

A The decorative *ristras* that you find in stores and souvenir shops across the Southwest are shellacked to a shiny finish for appearance and to make them last longer. Never eat chiles from this type of *ristra* or use them in your recipes. Even a good washing will not remove the protective coating. Culinary *ristras* may not look as bright, but they are the ones you want to add to your pot.

Q I love sun-dried tomatoes in oil. How can I make those at home?

A Tomatoes in oil are delicious — the oil softens the dried fruit and flavors the oil so you get two great-tasting products out of one. But if you are going to store your tomatoes in oil, you must be very careful. Dried tomatoes — whether you dry them in the sun, oven, or dehydrator — that are packed in oil *must be refrigerated and consumed within 2 weeks*. The oil creates a perfect vector for contamination, so it is imperative that these treats be handled carefully. Never leave the jar on the counter or cupboard for storage. There are no safe home-canning processes for this product.

Q What are some good ways to use dried foods?

A Dried fruits have so many great uses. They can be eaten out of hand, tossed into salads, or reconstituted in a little brandy and served over ice cream. Dried vegetables are great added to stews and soups or rehydrated and added to casseroles. One of my favorite tricks for dried items such as citrus zest, mushrooms, and chile peppers is to turn them into dust by pulverizing them in a cleaned coffee grinder. The dust can then be used as a seasoning in baked goods such as breads and as a thickener in long-cooking recipes. Mushroom dust is great in risotto, where it brings a rich, earthy flavor. Citrus dust can be sprinkled on a salad or stirred into cookie dough. Chile dust is just another name for chili powder, like ancho chile pepper that is sometimes seen on the spice rack. Use your homemade chile dust as you would any pure ground chili powder; it tastes great in chili, of course, and also sprinkled on roasted potatoes or stirred into sauces and stews.

CHAPTER 10

Fermentation

Some of our most delicious foods are fermented. Beer, wine, cheese, and good bread are all the tasty results of a good ferment. Who knew controlled rot could be so delectable? Not only are they palate pleasers, but fermented foods are also loaded with probiotics, the beneficial bacteria that populate a healthy gut. Our modern diet doesn't include as many fermented foods as it once did, and even foods that are fermented are often pasteurized, a process that destroys the active probiotics. But you can have these good bugs back in your diet. Just make fermented foods yourself. Here are some of the most popular questions I've been asked about fermenting.

Encouraging a Good Ferment

Q Fermentation seems so mysterious. How does it work?

A Fermenting is one of the oldest forms of food preservation and is really simple to do. It's a process that happens naturally — one that you can accomplish with no special training or specialized equipment. Here's how it works.

Essentially, you are just encouraging the natural lactic acid bacteria found on all produce to proliferate. As they do, they create the lactic acid that flavors and lowers the pH of your recipe to an acidic level that protects your food during storage. Salt — either sprinkled on chopped or shredded produce or mixed with water to form a brine — is frequently added to abate any contaminating bacteria, molds, or fungi.

Between the lactic acid that is generated and the salt that is added to the mixture, the ferment is very inhospitable to pathogens, making fermentation a safe and delicious way to preserve food. Try the recipe for sauerkraut on page 162 and you will see just how easy the process can be.

Q What is lactic acid? Do I need to add it to the crock?

A Lactic acid is created by the fermentation process. Unlike acetic acid, also known as vinegar, you do not need to add it to the crock. It results naturally as the beneficial lactic acid bacteria that are ever-present on produce digest the sugars in the fruits and vegetables and generate the lactic acid.

Q Why didn't my pickles ferment?

A There are a few factors that can keep a ferment from taking off. Here are two of the most common:

Too cold. Cool temperatures will slow, or even prevent, fermentation. You can use this to your benefit by placing your crock in a cool basement in the summer months to slow down the fermenting action. But the room temperature shouldn't be so cold that you would call it chilly — it should be a comfortable to cool room temperature for ideal fermentation.

Too strong. If you add too much salt to your pickle brine, you can halt fermentation. Some salt controls bacteria, but too much will halt the active bacteria that keep the ferment moving along. You should use a little less than 1 tablespoon of kosher salt per 1 cup of water, or about 3 tablespoons for every quart.

Q My fermented pickles have a thick white layer on the bottom of the jar. Is that okay?

A A thickish white layer on the bottom of the jar is most likely made up of dead yeast that has settled in the bottom of the jar. You will notice this at the bottom of kombucha (fermented tea) and other fermented products as well. It is not harmful and is a natural by-product of the fermentation process.

A white film on top of your ferment should be removed. This is a layer of yeasts and molds that are trying to set up house in your crock and, while not harmful if removed, can upset the balance of your ferment if left to proliferate into a thick pad. Check your fermentation crock regularly and gently dip off this "bloom" as it develops. Be sure to replace any liquid lost in its removal by topping up your jar with enough brine to cover your produce (just under 1 tablespoon of kosher salt dissolved in 1 cup of water).

CLASSIC FERMENTED SAUERKRAUT

Makes 2 quarts

This is one of my favorite recipes to demo: It's part science exper-iment and part tasty recipe; and it is a great lesson in the magic of beneficial bacteria, for kids and adults alike! In a world full of endless ingredient lists on packaged foods, it's amazing how much flavor you will get out of just a few humble items. A useful, though not essential, device for this recipe is a kraut board — a traditional tool for shredding cabbage, similar to a wooden mandoline.

INGREDIENTS

5 pounds green or red cabbage, or a combination
   (1 large head or 2 small)

5 tablespoons kosher salt

1 tablespoon juniper berries or caraway seeds (optional)

PREPARE

1. Peel away the outer leaves of the cabbage, and then quarter and core. Shred it finely using a knife, mandoline, or kraut board. Toss with the salt and the juniper berries, if using, in a large nonreactive bowl until thoroughly combined. Transfer to a 1-gallon glass jar or ceramic crock and press down. Top the cabbage with a clean plate, just smaller than the opening of the jar. Fill a clean quart jar with water and use it to weight down the plate. Cover with a clean tea towel and transfer to a cool place.

2. Check the kraut after 24 hours. With the help of the plate, all the cabbage should be submerged. If it's not, pour enough brine (1 tablespoon of salt to 1 cup of water) over the cabbage to cover it.

3. Check the cabbage daily. Tiny bubbles should be rising through the liquid (easy to see in a glass container). If a scum has formed, don't worry; just ladle it from the top of the liquid and wash and replace the plate and water-filled jar. Add more brine, if necessary, to keep the cabbage submerged. The kraut will be fully fermented in 1 to 2 weeks at room temperature or 3 to 4 weeks in a cool basement. You'll know it's done when it stops bubbling and is a pale golden color.

PRESERVE

Refrigerate: Store in the refrigerator, covered, for up to 1 month.

Q Some of my produce is poking out of the top of the ferment. Is that okay?

A It's very important that all of the produce that you wish to ferment is submerged under the brine. Food that is exposed to air, and airborne pathogens, is likely to rot rather than pickle. Use a clean plate just smaller than the opening of your container to weight your produce down and keep it well covered with liquid.

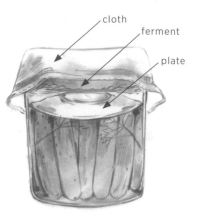

cloth
ferment
plate

fermentation setup

Q My ferment is evaporating. What can I do?

A It is not uncommon for some of the brine to evaporate during fermentation. But it is important that your food stay submerged. If you notice your brine is getting low, you can top it up with a solution of just under 1 tablespoon of kosher salt dissolved in 1 cup of water.

Q My ferment is bubbling. Has it gone bad?

A Bubbles occur naturally in the fermentation process and are a good sign that things are going well. As the sugars are converted into lactic acid and acetic acid, carbon dioxide is created and sometimes appears as bubbles in the crock. As the process nears its end and your kraut or pickles are finishing their fermentation, the bubbling action will slow.

Q There is mold on top of my ferment. Is it rotten?

A It is not uncommon for a cap of mold, or bloom, to form on the top of your ferment. This is particularly common in the beginning stages of fermentation, when the process hasn't yet had time to create enough lactic acid to lower the pH of the brine.

If you notice a patch of mold or bloom floating on top of your crock, just gently scoop it off. Wash the plate or container you are using to weight down your produce. Top off your brine if necessary by dissolving a little less than 1 tablespoon of kosher salt in 1 cup of water and adding it to your ferment.

Q How can I test to see if my fermented foods are ready?

A The best tool for testing the readiness of your fermented food is your taste buds. Don't be afraid to try the food as it moves through the fermentation process — it's not harmful to eat the food at any stage. After about a week or so, you can remove a cucumber from your brine, slice it in half, and look inside (even sooner if you are fermenting in the heat of the summer, when the process goes much more quickly). It should be fairly uniform in texture, with no unfermented core at its center. If it looks good, give it a nibble. If it is pleasantly tart to you, you are done. If you would like the pickles to have a bit more pep, leave them for a few more days. When they taste as tangy as you want, put them in the fridge, submerged in their brine. Keep in mind that they will continue to pick up flavors from the brine as they sit in the fridge. And, although the cold of the icebox will slow fermentation, it won't completely stop it. So your pickles or kraut will get a little stronger with age.

Q How much water should I add to my sauerkraut brine?

A Sauerkraut uses the dry salting method — the chopped or shredded produce is tossed with salt, which leaches liquid out of the cabbage, creating its own brine. Only if you have a particularly dry head of cabbage, do you need to add any liquid at all. If after 24 hours your shredded, salted cabbage has not released enough liquid to be submerged, you can top off the jar with a little brine. To make the brine, dissolve 1 scant tablespoon of kosher salt in 1 cup of water.

Never add plain water to fermenting foods. It will dilute the salinity of the brine, which may lead to less desirable results.

making sauerkraut

Q A mouse died in my crock. How can I keep that from happening?

A It is really important to cover your crock so that pests cannot snack and/or swim on or in your ferment. The best way to do this is to drape a tea towel or double thickness of cheesecloth over the top of the crock and then secure it with a rubber band or similar band to keep it tightly fitted around the top of the container. Alternatively, I have heard from fermenters that they have fashioned a stainless steel screen that fits the top of their crock, which allows air in and keeps pests out. Either way, you don't want visitors in there, so cover it up.

Q Wow, this stuff is smelly! Is that okay?

A Beauty is in the eye of the beholder, I suppose. Fermenting vegetables do have a strong smell. Some love it and others, not so much. But if you think the fermenting crock is fragrant, you should put your nose in my cheese drawer. *Woof!* I would suggest that when fermented foods played a larger role in our diets, we were more accustomed to the way they smelled and weren't as put off. Perhaps once you get in the fermenting habit, you will feel the same. Until then, if you need the slow ramp-up on the fermenting fumes, you might consider putting your crock in the garage to do its work. Who knows — maybe eventually, it will be invited inside to stay.

Kitchen Tip

If you have never fermented before, use a glass jar rather than a clay crock, at least for your first few rounds. It allows you to see what's going on inside the ferment so that you can better understand the process (and enjoy the kitchen science).

Equipment

Q What kind of container is suitable for fermenting?

A Never use anything but a food-grade container for fermenting. Glass, ceramic, or food-grade plastic is fine. Never use a recycled container — such as a paint bucket — for fermenting. Such containers can transfer trace amounts of their previous contents or leach chemicals from the plastic itself into your food.

Q I live in an apartment in New York City. Can I ferment foods in my kitchen or do you need a basement?

A Many eaters ferment in their basements, where the cool, constant temperatures make it easier to regulate the fermentation process. But a basement or even cool temperatures aren't necessary to successfully ferment your produce. In fact, some practitioners of the process swear by the antiseptic action of strong sunlight and always set their crock where it can catch some rays. If you are fermenting in your kitchen, or anywhere where the temperatures will be 70°F and above, you might add a bit more salt to your mix, as it will slow the process considerably.

It is easiest to control a ferment in an environment that is not subject to extreme temperatures. A hot kitchen in the middle of August may not be the best. But you don't need a basement to ferment your own food, and many of my city friends do just fine at a normal room temperature of 68°F or so. Just keep in mind that higher temperatures will speed fermentation and cold temps will slow it down.

Ingredients

Q I've heard that you can use leaves to keep fermented pickles crisp. Is this true?

A Not only *can* you use leaves to keep your fermented pickles crisp, but it's one of the best tricks in the book. The leaves to use are those that contain tannins, such as oak, cherry, and grape leaves. Don't use too many or the tannic taste — which is responsible for that dry-mouth flavor of over-brewed tea — will overpower your pickles. A small handful — three or four large leaves, or up to six small ones — will crisp your pickles without throwing off the flavor of your brine. I ferment in a clear glass jar and the leaves, mixed in with the garlic, spices, and cucumbers, look great, too.

Q What kind of salt should I use for fermenting?

A As with all food-preserving processes, you want to use salt without any additives, which can affect the color or flavor of your foods. Ordinary table salt is often treated with anti-caking agents to help it flow more freely in the shaker, and iodine, a dietary supplement. I use kosher salt for all of my preserving recipes — it's readily available and additive-free. Some preservers swear by the nutritive benefits of sea salt and prefer to use that in their recipes. I would avoid sea salts that contain high amounts of minerals — such as black salt — that could interfere with your results. Save these flavorful and gorgeous salts for seasoning foods on the plate. (See A Glossary of Salt, page 55.)

Q I am on a low-salt diet. Can I use a salt substitute in my ferments?

A Salt plays such an important role in fermentation, keeping pathogens at bay so that the beneficial bacteria can do their work of creating the lactic acid that pickles the produce. While you don't need to use specialized canning salt to get good results, fermenting without any salt would be tricky at best, and it is not recommended by the USDA.

That being said, Sandor Katz, who is a well-regarded authority on fermentation, suggests that you can ferment using wine, herbs, and seaweed as alternatives to salt to control contaminating pathogens.

Q Can you ferment fruit?

A Sure — it's called wine! The high sugar content of fruit makes it hard to ferment without turning into alcohol. It can be done, however. Moroccan pickled lemons are one example. The fruit is cut and filled with salt and then packed tightly into jars and allowed to cure in the sun until the skins are softened. The salt flavor is strong, though, so it is usually rinsed off the fruit before the lemons are used in recipes.

Q I would like to add some different vegetables to my sauerkraut. Is that okay?

A Fermentation isn't just for cabbage and cucumbers. Lots of vegetables taste great when fermented and can be used instead of, or in addition to, your kraut recipes. Carrots, ginger, radishes, and daikon are just a few that come to mind that would be particularly tasty in a sauerkraut preparation. I recommend shredding them either in a food processor or on a mandoline to ensure that the cabbage and added vegetables ferment evenly.

Just be sure that whatever produce you use, it remains completely submerged under the brine during the fermentation process. If the mixture you choose does not exude enough liquid to create its own brine, top off your crock with a mixture of just under 1 tablespoon of kosher salt dissolved in 1 cup of water.

Q What kind of water is best for fermenting?

A If your tap water is suitable for drinking, you can use it for fermenting. If you live in an area where the water is heavily chlorinated, you might consider boiling it and bringing it to room temperature to evaporate the chlorine before proceeding with your recipe. You can also use bottled or distilled water for fermenting.

Q How do I know whether I should salt my produce or add a brine to ferment it?

A Sprinkling your produce with salt, also known as *dry salting*, extracts the natural juices from produce to create its own brine. It's a process generally used for chopped or shredded fruits or vegetables, where the high ratio of surface area allows the salt to act on the produce quickly. The salt draws out the juices and the produce is effectively submerged under brine created by its own liquid.

Foods that are submerged under liquid brine are often those that are left whole, such as cucumbers. Due to their large size, it would be hard to encourage these foods to release enough of their own liquid to submerge them in the crock. To create a fermenting brine, dissolve kosher salt in water in a ratio of 1 scant tablespoon of kosher salt in 1 cup of water.

Q How do I know how much brine to use?

A You need to completely submerge your produce under the brine for it to be effective. But the volume that you make depends solely on the amount of produce you are fermenting and the size of your crock. You don't have to think of it as an exact science; just mix up a batch and pour it into the crock. You can add more if you need to get the produce well submerged. As long as you stick to a ratio of just under 1 tablespoon of salt to every cup of water, you can scale the volume as you need.

Q Can I use different spices in my fermented foods?

A Yes, you can use spices to change the flavors of your fermented foods. Many different cultures have their signature combinations. Kimchi uses chiles and ginger. Caraway is a popular addition to sauerkraut in Germany. But you can feel free to experiment. Try peppercorns, coriander seeds, juniper berries, or a few cloves. Keep in mind that mild flavors, such as lemongrass, may become subsumed by the strong flavors of fermented foods.

Some spices, such as turmeric, are antimicrobial. This will not affect the ferment, however; the lactic acid bacteria working to keep the food safe and give it its signature tang is a hardy breed.

In fact, such spices can actually help the process by staving off contaminating molds.

Q Can I add raw fish to my kimchi to flavor it?

A Raw fish is a traditional addition to kimchi that gives it a signature *umami*, or earthy, meaty, flavor. If the prospect of using raw fish in the mix is a bit daunting, you can still get the earthy flavor with some less intimidating ingredients. Try a small amount of dried shrimp (available in Asian markets), anchovy paste, or even Worcestershire sauce, which contains anchovies as one of its main flavoring components. Vegans and vegetarians might consider a bit of rehydrated seaweed in the mix to get a similar flavor without any animal products.

Q How salty should my brine be?

A Fermentation is not an exact science. There are guidelines for success, but not a precise formula; much of it is a matter of taste. One traditional rule is that your brine should be strong enough to float an egg. But if you have ever tasted such a brine — or food prepared with it — you might agree that this amount of salt is too intense for modern tastes. A 5 percent brine will get the job done and is more in tune with modern palates. This means that you are using 5 percent of salt to water, by weight. Varying salt grains will give you different weights per measure — the finer the grain, the heavier it is by volume — but a good rule of thumb is just under 1 tablespoon of kosher salt per 1 cup of water, or 3 tablespoons of salt per 1 quart of water. You can lower the salt a bit, and doing so will speed your fermentation process. You can increase it, too, and that will slow the fermentation.

Q Why are my pickles hollow?

A Hollow pickles can be caused by a number of different things. One of the most common reasons for a hollow pickle is that they were pickled too long after harvest. It's important that cucumbers make their way to the fermentation crock as soon after picking as possible. Even a day or two can lead to disappointing results. Another reason is that the cucumbers may have been left too long on the vine. Old cucumbers will have a hollow core, which can be hard to detect when you are fermenting them whole. Use produce that is at its peak of ripeness for fermenting.

Q I have some grapevines in my backyard. Can I pickle the leaves?

A Absolutely! Pickled grape leaves are delicious when stuffed with all manner of different fillings. The best leaves to use are the young, tender spring leaves. Pick them just when they get big enough to hold a bit of filling. Opt for the leaves of white grapes, which are more succulent than the leaves of red grapes.

The best way to preserve them is to ferment them. Make a stack of 12 leaves and roll them up like a cigar. Repeat with 24 leaves to make 2 more rolls, packing them in a clean quart glass jar as you go. Submerge them under a simple brine of 1 scant tablespoon of kosher salt dissolved in each 1 cup of water. Weight down with a small jar and cover with a tea towel. Allow to ferment until the leaves are pliable and tangy, about 1 week. Refrigerate until ready to use.

Storage

Q Can I can my fermented foods?

A Technically, yes, you may can fermented foods. The lactic acid that forms in the process will drop the pH low enough for fermented foods to be processed using the boiling-water method.

However, the heat of the canning process destroys one of the best benefits of fermented foods: the beneficial bacteria created during the process. This beneficial bacteria, like that in yogurt, is terrific for your digestion. Probiotic foods like fermented pickles and krauts, and yogurt and kefir, have long been valued in traditional cuisines for their multiple health benefits and are gaining popularity in modern science's approach to health. Refrigerate these products to prolong their shelf life and enjoy them, as they are — alive and well.

Q I have my fermented pickles in the refrigerator. That stops the fermentation, right?

A Actually, refrigeration only slows fermentation; it doesn't stop it. Your pickles, kraut, or kimchi will continue to ferment, but at a greatly reduced rate. Be sure to check the jar periodically, dipping off any bloom that forms on top of the brine. Top up the brine as necessary to keep all produce fully submerged.

Q Can I cook with fermented food?

A You can, but keep in mind that one of the biggest benefits of enjoying fermented foods is the probiotics that they provide. These beneficial bacteria cannot survive heat, so any cooking will destroy them. The food will still taste good, but it won't pack the probiotic punch of raw, fermented foods.

CHAPTER 11

Infusions

Alcohol and vinegar both make great canvases that take on the flavor of the produce you infuse in them. And all of those decorative jars that you can't use to can? Well, this is the perfect use for them. Mix up a batch of infusions during the summer and you will have a treasure trove of holiday gifts to give. In this chapter, you'll find some of the basic things you need to know to get started creating your own delicious infusions.

Q I love flavored oils. Can I submerge basil in oil to flavor it?

A We have all seen those decorative containers of herbs and sometimes garlic cloves, vegetables, or spices encased in oil, and maybe you have thought, I can make those. Don't do it! Herbs and vegetables are not acidic. Submerging them in oil creates precisely the kind of nonacidic, anaerobic environment that is the perfect breeding ground for botulism. Any flavored oils that you make should be refrigerated for short-term storage or kept in the freezer if you want to store them for more than a few days.

Q Can I eat the fruit in my alcohol infusions?

A Yes, you can, if you are of legal drinking age. The fruit in alcohol infusions gives up a lot of its flavor to the booze and, in turn, absorbs a lot of booze in the process. So, the produce will be quite potent. Keeping that in mind, you can make a lovely grown-up dessert by spooning some of the fruit from your infusion over ice cream, meringues, or pound cake — delicious, if a bit dangerous! You can also blend the fruit into frozen cocktails. Think of it as a smoothie for the older set.

Q What is the best alcohol to use for a liquor infusion?

A Most liquor infusions are made with high-proof spirits, such as 80-proof vodka, which ensures that your infusion will remain stable and will not ferment. If you do notice any bubbling in your infusion, you can top it off with a little grain alcohol or overproof rum to bring it back to balance.

I have infused lower-alcohol libations, such as sake and wine. Just be sure to refrigerate these products and use them within the time indicated in your recipe.

Q Should I sterilize my bottles before adding my infusion ingredients?

A You will find mixed opinions about sterilizing bottles before using them to hold infusions. I think, why not? It's easy enough — you just dunk your clean bottle or jar into boiling water for 10 minutes — and it gives you an extra edge over any potentially contaminating elements that would jeopardize your good work. So, if you can, presterilize.

There are instances, however, when you cannot presterilize. When you are working with a crock or other large container that is too big to submerge, for example, you have to do the best you can. In these instances, I recommend the following:

1. Scrub out your container with dish soap to remove any grease or dirt. Rinse thoroughly.

2. Scrub with salt to remove any soap film or fragrance.

3. Rinse with boiling water.

4. Finally, rinse out the container with a small amount of infusion base — either vinegar or alcohol — to eradicate any lingering baddies.

If you are going to go through the time, effort, and expense of creating a large batch of infusion, you don't want to run the risk of contamination because the vessel wasn't quite clean. It takes a little time, but after you are through, your container will be as clean as a whistle.

Q What kind of container is best for storing infusions?

A Infusions should be made and stored only in food-grade nonreactive containers, such as glass or ceramic meant for food. Be careful of ceramic glazes that may contain lead, and ditto any crystal vessel. Such containers may look gorgeous but will leach toxic elements into your recipe — not good.

Q Should I heat the booze before adding it to the jar?

A Never heat alcohol on the stove. High-alcohol liquids can easily catch on fire, creating a very dangerous situation. The spirits have enough firepower of their own; just add them straight to your clean, sterilized jar.

Kitchen Tip

Sweetened infused vinegars make refreshing spritzers. Add a few tablespoons to a glass of seltzer water for a refreshing, light drink known as a *shrub*.

Q Can I use sweeteners other than sugar?

A Sugar is sometimes added to an infusion before or after the process. If it is added before, it helps the fruit to maintain its shape. Sugar hardens the cell walls of produce, so it will keep your cherries, for example, from just turning to mush.

When sugar is added after the infusion, it is done so as a flavoring. In this case, it is fine to substitute another sweetener, such as honey or agave syrup.

Q I have a thin layer of murky sediment on the bottom of my infusion. What should I do?

A It's not unusual to have a thin layer of sediment on the bottom of an infusion. Even after you strain out the fruit, some particulates remain and will settle out on the bottom of your container after a time. It's harmless, but if you find it unsightly, it's easy enough to take care of. Gently pour off the clear infusion into another container, leaving the sediment behind. Wash out your original container and return your now crystal-clear liquid to it.

Q What kind of vinegar should I use for flavored vinegars?

A Think of your vinegar as a canvas — it's okay if it has a little texture, but you really want a clean slate. Avoid richly flavored vinegars, such as malt vinegar, that will mask the flavor of your infusing ingredients. Stick to neutral-flavored vinegars like distilled white vinegar, apple cider vinegar, or white wine vinegar. Keep in mind that flavored vinegars can be sweetened to take the edge off of sharp flavors if necessary.

STRAWBERRY VINEGAR

Makes about 3 cups

Strawberries give this infusion a sweet, fresh taste and a very rich red color. You can leave it unsweetened if you prefer. Either way, it is terrific for dressing salads, brightening a platter of grilled meats, and more. Feel free to substitute any berry you have on hand — they all make terrific infusions.

INGREDIENTS

1 pint strawberries, hulled and halved

2 cups distilled white vinegar

½ cup sugar

PREPARE

1. Sterilize a quart jar by submerging it in boiling water for 10 minutes.

2. Add berries and vinegar to the clean, hot jar. Top with a square of waxed or parchment paper to prevent direct contact with the lid, then screw on the lid. Give it a good shake and set aside in a cool, dark place for 2 weeks, shaking every day or so.

3. Strain the berries and discard the fruit. Resterilize the jar.

4. Bring the infused vinegar to a boil and add sugar, stirring to dissolve. Pour the vinegar into the prepared jar and let cool. Cover and store in a cool, dark place for up to 1 year.

PART 3

Putting Your Skills to Work

*T*hink of this section as the recipe fixer. In it you'll find information that is specific to distinct food preparations. Can't get your jam to gel? Check out Sweet and Savory Spreads. Need a recipe for Pickling Spice? You will find it and more in Pickles. Sauces will help you keep your ketchup from separating. Vegetables will help you keep your produce wholesome. Whole Fruits offers tips for avoiding the dreaded fruit float. Tomatoes and Tomato Products covers everything you want to do with the fruit, from saucing it to making it into salsa to canning it whole. These pointers and more will ensure that your recipes turn out wholesome and tasty every time.

CHAPTER 12

Sweet and Savory Spreads

Spreads are a wide category of canned foods that include all the recipes that are expected to gel. Jams, jellies, compotes, conserves, preserves, and marmalades are all covered in this section. They are scrumptious and gorgeous and, for many, a favorite way to preserve field-fresh foods. My favorite spreads are those that teeter on the seesaw between sweet and savory. Jellies with a peppery kick, vegetable jams, and gingery preserves are not only something a beat apart to have on your pantry shelf, but they also serve double-duty by sidling up to breakfast breads in the morning and an after-dinner cheese plate at night. Whether you prefer to make your spreads sweet or savory, here are some tips for making them just right.

Basics

Q What's the difference between a jam and a jelly?

A Jams and jellies are both sweet fruit spreads, but differ in texture. Jams are made with mashed fruit, with some pieces still intact. Jellies, on the other hand, are made solely from the fruit's juice. Crystal clear and sparkling, they are the true beauties of the canning kitchen. (See Learn the Lingo, page 18.) The best fruits for jellies are those that are abundantly juicy and readily give off their liquid. Canners often make jelly out of highly seeded fruits as well, as the pips are removed in the juice extraction process. For these reasons and more, raspberries and grapes are good candidates for jelly.

Jams and jellies both have a thick, spreadable consistency that can be achieved by using either the quick or classic cooking method described next.

Q What's the difference between quick-cook and long-cook jams (besides the cooking time)?

A The difference between quick-cooking and long-cooking jams comes down to pectin, the substance that thickens spreads as they cook. Quick-cook jams have commercial pectin, found in liquid or powder form, added to them to achieve a gel. Long-cook jams — also called classic jams — rely on the fruit's natural pectin, which combines with the acid and sugar in the recipe, to reach the gel stage.

Because of their short time on the stove, quick-cooking jams often have a more fruit-forward flavor than long-cooking spreads. The use of commercial pectin, however, can give these spreads a bit of a gelatinous, Jell-O kind of texture. There is no guesswork in making a quick-cooking jam; just prepare your recipe and process as directed and your spread will set as it cools in your jars.

With their extended time on the stovetop, long-cooking jams have a rounder flavor than spreads that use added pectin to set. Utilizing the fruit's natural pectin results in a silky, viscous texture. It can be a little tricky to know when a long-cooking jam is at its perfect gelling stage, but it's a classic technique that is worth learning. (See Getting a Good Set, page 199.)

Q I love the idea of making homemade jam but don't have a lot of time. Is there a quick recipe you could recommend so I could give it a whirl?

A Sure! Jam making does not have to be an all-day endeavor, particularly if you use commercial pectin, rather than a long cooking time, to get your gel. One of the simplest jams to make is Quick Blueberry Jam (recipe follows). The blueberries require no peeling or pit removal, so they are easy to work with. Just give them a quick going over to remove any stray stems and a good wash and you are ready to go.

Q What's the point of skimming jam?

A The bubbling action of boiling jam can leave foam on its surface when the cooking is done. The foam is not harmful, but it has a cottony, unpleasant mouthfeel after it sets up, so it's best to remove it. Give your jam a few minutes to rest after cooking, stirring

QUICK BLUEBERRY JAM

Makes about 4 cups

The fruit in this jam requires virtually no prep, and the added pectin means that it sets up in a flash. This is a terrific gift idea. You can make up cases of it in no time, and you'll have all of your holiday shopping done . . . in August!

INGREDIENTS

4 cups sugar

2 teaspoons Pomona's Universal Pectin

8 cups blueberries, stemmed

¼ cup bottled lemon juice

2 teaspoons calcium water
   (included in the Pomona box)

PREPARE

1. Combine the sugar and pectin in a small bowl and set aside. Combine the berries with a splash of water in a medium nonreactive saucepan and slowly bring to a boil over low heat. Add the lemon juice and calcium water. Pour in the sugar-pectin mixture and stir to dissolve.

2. Return to a boil, and then immediately remove from the heat and let the jam rest for 5 minutes, stirring occasionally to release air bubbles. Skim off any foam.

PRESERVE

Refrigerate: Ladle into bowls or jars. Let cool, cover, and refrigerate. Jam keeps covered for up to 3 weeks.

Can: Use the boiling-water method (see page 95). Pour into clean, hot 4-ounce or half-pint canning jars, leaving ¼ inch of headspace. Use a bubble tool, or other nonmetallic implement, to release any trapped air. Wipe the rims, cover the jars, and screw the bands on just fingertip-tight. Process for 10 minutes. Cool for 24 hours. Check the seals and store in a cool, dark place for up to 1 year.

occasionally, to give any trapped air a chance to dissipate. Then simply dip the edge of a large spoon or ladle just below the surface of the jam and drag it across the top of the mixture. You can sort of corral the foam along the side of your pot and then scoop it out a spoonful at a time. Some canners choose to add a dot of butter or margarine to the pot to keep foaming to a minimum, but it's not a practice I follow.

Q Can I add some butter to my jam to avoid foaming?

A Many canners add a pat of butter or margarine to their jam pot to keep foam from forming. I am not a fan of this practice for a few different reasons:

- It makes it much harder to get the rim of the jar clean, which can lead to seal failure.

- I don't like the idea of storing fat on the shelf for up to a year.

- If you add butter to the pan, the product no longer qualifies as vegan, so you will have to label or explain this typically animal-free product before serving or gifting it.

Q My grandmother used to use paraffin to seal her jams. Can I do that?

A Jars of jam sealed with paraffin are adorable but not very reliable. Without the sealing step that the boiling-water method provides, it's easy for bacteria and other contaminants to find their way into the preserves before the paraffin is ladled over the top. And a hot day is apt to loosen the paraffin as well, providing another opportunity for spoilage. I know canners who still swear by this method and seal their jars with melted wax. They admit that occasionally they will peel back the paraffin and find their preserves covered with a furry layer of mold on top. They peel that off and dig in, but I don't advise it. Beard on a man? Charming. On your jam? Not so much.

Q What's the point of adding water to my jam recipe if I'm just going to cook it all away anyway?

A When you are cooking recipes for an extended period of time, such as classic jams, chutneys, and marmalades, water equals time; it gives your food enough time in the pot to simmer until it reaches the desired texture. Without the added water, your recipe would scorch before the fruit became tender. If you find that your produce needs to soften a bit more — if your citrus peels are still too stiff for your liking, for example — you can always add a little splash of water and simmer for a bit more time until you hit your target.

Q I get my jam really hot before I put it in the jars. Then I just turn them over. I get a good seal, so it's okay that I don't process them, right?

A A seal is not the only goal of proper processing. The boiling-water method, which processes unsterilized, filled jars by submerging them in boiling water for at least 10 minutes, ensures not only that you will get a vacuum seal, but also that any lingering bacteria in the jar or headspace will be destroyed. Without this step, you may get a seal, but you may not have killed potential pathogens than can spoil your jam. Always process your jars for the full amount of time indicated in your recipe for the best results.

Q Which fruits are best for making jelly?

A Jelly can be a time-consuming process, so I reserve it for fruits that will truly benefit from the gentle juice extraction it requires. Fruits that have too many pips for my taste are great candidates for jelly making, which will strain them out. I also use it for very juicy fruits, such as watermelon and tomatoes, that give up their abundant liquids easily. If you find berries too pricey for jelly making, you can include a few apples in the pot. They are relatively inexpensive and will increase your jelly yield while their mild flavor lets the berry taste shine through.

Q I love to make homemade jams, but there's only so much toast a body can eat. Any other uses?

A Absolutely! You don't have to limit your jams and jellies to the breakfast table. Your spreads can be used in a variety of recipes, both sweet and savory. I use my jams and jellies to fill cookies and cakes for a sweet treat. I whisk them into my vinaigrettes; they give the dressings a lovely, deep tone and a little extra body that helps it cling to fresh greens. But one of my favorite tricks is to whisk the

PAN-ROASTED CHICKEN WITH RASPBERRY REDUCTION

Serves 4 to 6

Making a pan reduction is a great trick to have up your culinary sleeve. You can use this same method for making a sauce out of any pan-roasted meat. Feel free to substitute different kinds of spreads as well — blueberry jelly would be very nice, and cherry jelly would work particularly well, too.

INGREDIENTS

1 chicken, cut into 10 pieces
   (breasts halved; wings and back reserved for stock)

2 teaspoons kosher salt

1 tablespoon unsalted butter

1 tablespoon extra-virgin olive oil

1 shallot, finely diced

1 tablespoon all-purpose flour

1 cup dry white wine

1 cup chicken stock, preferably homemade

   Pinch of dried thyme

   Freshly ground black pepper

2 tablespoons raspberry jelly

PREPARE

1. Preheat the oven to 375°F. Using paper towels, dry the chicken pieces thoroughly. Sprinkle with the salt.

2. Heat the butter and oil in a large ovenproof skillet over medium-high heat. Add the chicken, putting the thickest pieces in the center of the pan, and sauté until the skin has darkened to a deep golden brown and the pieces easily release from the pan. Using tongs, turn the chicken pieces over and slide the pan onto the center rack of the oven. Roast for about 20 minutes, until the internal temperature reaches 165°F. Transfer the chicken to a platter, lower the oven temperature to warm, and set the chicken in the warm oven. (Do not cover the chicken or the skin will lose its crispness.)

3. Drain off all but 2 tablespoons of the fat in the skillet. Return the skillet to the heat, add the shallot, and sauté until it is translucent, about 2 minutes. Whisk in the flour and then the wine. Simmer until thickened, about 5 minutes. Add the stock, thyme, and pepper to taste, and simmer until reduced and slightly thickened, 2 to 3 minutes. Add the jelly and whisk to dissolve.

4. Ladle the sauce onto a high-sided serving platter and top with the chicken pieces (ladling sauce over chicken would cover up and soften the gorgeous brown skin). Serve immediately.

preserves into a pan reduction for an instant, elegant sauce. Try the recipe on page 186, but feel free to improvise with your own combinations.

Q Is fruit cheese an animal product?

A No, fruit cheese is another name for fruit butter that has been cooked down for so long that it can be molded into a shape. It has no animal products in it, so it is completely vegan. Quince is used to make a very popular fruit cheese called *membrillo*. The fruit is cooked down with sugar until it almost resembles a dough, pulling away from the sides of the pot as you stir it. Then it is transferred to a loaf pan lined with oiled plastic wrap or parchment paper and refrigerated. After it cools, the cheese can be unmolded and sliced for serving.

Q I love making jam but I am kind of tired of my recipes. Any tricks?

A I am crazy about spreads that bring a little kick to the party. A little ground dried chile can be added to many jams for a savory twist. Add it in the last moment of cooking so it will have enough time to release its gorgeous flavor to your jam but not enough time to fill your kitchen with eye-stinging steam. You can add other savory spices to your spreads as well. Here are a few tasty combinations to try:

- peach + smoked paprika
- apricot + ginger
- cherry + black pepper
- lemon marmalade + oregano
- orange marmalade + thyme
- plum + cardamom

Q Can I substitute other citrus fruits in my marmalade recipes?

A You can make marmalade out of most citrus fruits, but a recipe that is appropriate for one kind of fruit may not be suitable for another. While the basic techniques might apply across the board, there are issues of preparation and timing that can be unique to the fruit. Citrus fruits have a range of bitterness that needs to be taken into account. Variations in skin thickness can also lead to overcooked or tough textures if a swap is made. Marmalade recipes often give a small list of fruits that are suitable for substitution. If the fruit you want to cure is not listed, it's best to find a recipe that was designed specifically for it.

Q Is it safe to can lemon curd using the boiling-water method? I thought you needed a pressure canner for preserving protein, and my recipe has a lot of eggs in it.

A Counterintuitive as it is, it is perfectly safe to can citrus curd. The lemon juice gives the recipe all of the acid it needs to stay safe on the shelf. That doesn't mean that it isn't tricky. Use a thermometer to make sure that your mixture comes to temperature before ladling it into your jars — 160°F tells you not only that you have reached the thickening point but also that you have pasteurized your mixture. Process promptly and only for 10 minutes for 4- or 8-ounce jars. Any longer and you may scramble your eggs. Curd has a tendency to separate during storage. While I have had jars on the shelf for longer, you shouldn't count on the curd maintaining its delicate texture for more than 3 months. Too fussy for you? You can refrigerate your glorious curds for up to 3 weeks.

Equipment

Q I would love to make my jam in a gorgeous copper confiture, but isn't that kind of pot reactive?

A Yes! Copper is reactive, and cooking in an unlined pan can be dangerous. Fruit is acidic and can react with the pan in a way that is toxic. To avoid this risk, it is imperative that the fruit and sugar be combined in a bowl before being added to the copper pot. The sugar keeps the fruit from reacting with the pan. Never add the fruit first and never let your fruit soak or

Kitchen Tip

After a session of making preserves, your equipment can be covered with a good case of the gooey. For a quick cleanup, load all of the sticky things into your dirty jam pot. Pour the hot water from your canner over all. The hot water will dissolve the sugary residue instantly, and everything will then wash up quickly and easily.

macerate overnight in the copper, as the time spent in the pan can leach contaminants into the spread.

Some jam makers swear by unlined copper for its ability to conduct heat, but I find it a drawback. It's much too easy to scorch jam in a confiture, where the lick of the flame seems to transfer almost directly to the fruit. Enameled cast iron is nonreactive and thick enough to give you steady, even cooking, and you don't need to follow any special steps to keep it from reacting with your food.

Q What is a jelly bag? Is there a substitute?

A A jelly bag is a pouch specifically designed to hold cooked fruit as it drains its juice for jelly. It fits into a frame that supports the fruit-filled bag and suspends it over a bowl to collect the juice. If you make a lot of

Kitchen Tip

For easier cleanup, flip your jelly bag inside out, so the seams are on the outside, before setting it in the frame.

jelly or are a stickler for perfectly clear spreads, you might look into getting one. It will give you the finest results, and you can carefully wash and reuse the bag.

You can get very fine results as well from straining your cooked fruit through a colander or strainer lined with a double or triple thickness of cheesecloth. Just set the lined and filled setup in a bowl to collect your juice. The cheesecloth will become matted with fruit and is not reusable.

jelly bag

cheesecloth-lined colander

Q Can I use a pressure canner for jam?

A Generally, jams are processed for about 10 minutes, some even less. As pressure canners need to vent for 10 minutes before you even begin to pressurize them, and then must be allowed to depressurize before opening them, the jam would be terribly overprocessed using this method. Use the boiling-water method to safely process your spreads.

Q The jellies I made look so pretty. Can't I put them in decorative jars for gift giving?

A Decorative jars. So tempting. I find traditional canning jars adorable, myself. And they aren't just cute; they are specially designed for the process. Their extra-thick glass stands up to the temperature shifts into and out of the boiling water, and their two-piece lids give you the vacuum seal that you need to keep your food safe on the shelf. Sterilize your pretty jars by submerging them in boiling water for 10 minutes and then use them for infusions and refrigerator pickles, where a vacuum seal isn't necessary.

Pectin

Q What is pectin?

A Pectin is the naturally occurring component found in produce that when combined with sugar and acid, gives spreads their thick, unctuous texture. Citrus and tart apples have the most pectin, and it is an extraction of the pectin from these fruits that serves as the base in many commercial pectins. You can count on fruits that are high in pectin to firm up nicely in the jam. Low-pectin fruits often need a boost of added pectin, in the form of a few citrus peels in the pot or a dose of packaged pectin, to achieve the desired consistency.

Q How long should I boil my jam after adding the pectin?

A Once you add your pectin you need to boil it only briefly — for a minute or two — to make sure that it is dissolved and evenly distributed throughout your recipe. Extended boiling can weaken or break your pectin, resulting in a very thin spread.

Q Which fruits have the most pectin?

A I think what you really want to know is, which fruits gel the most readily? Because the ability to gel results from a combination of pectin and acid, it's the mix of both in a fruit that makes it a good candidate for a classic jam — one that doesn't need added pectin to get the correct texture. The following list should help.

High (gels readily)

- Sour apples/ crabapples*
- Citrus*

- Concord grapes
- Cranberries

- Plums
- Quince

*Strongest gelling power

Medium (will gel given time and attention)

- Blueberries
- Cherries

- Peaches
- Ripe apples

- Strawberries

Low (hard to get a set without added pectin)

- Apricots
- Pears

- Raspberries
- Rhubarb

Q Is there a way to test how much pectin is in my fruit?

A You can use regular rubbing alcohol to test for the level of pectin in your fruit. In a small container with a lid, combine 1 teaspoon of the cooked fruit or fruit juice with 1 tablespoon rubbing alcohol, cover, and shake. If a solid mass is formed, there is sufficient pectin in the fruit to form a gel using the long-cooking method. If a solid mass does not form, you will need to use the fruit in a recipe that calls for commercial pectin to get a good gel. (Do not eat the tested fruit blob!)

Q Can I make my own pectin?

A Absolutely! And if you have a supply of tart apples or crabapples available, then I suggest you do. Preserves made with homemade pectin are smooth and silky. They take a little time to make, but the texture cannot be beat. See the details on page 194 — it's a very easy process. Give it a try!

Q When do you add the pectin to the recipe?

A That depends on the kind of pectin you are using. They are all different. You should follow your recipes for specific details on timing and quantities, but generally it breaks down like this:

Homemade pectin. Homemade pectin enhances the gelling of your sweet spreads in much the same way as natural pectin. That is, you have to cook your recipe for an extended time to reach the gel stage. Combine it with your fruit, then add the sugar and lemon juice. Simmer until the gel stage is reached (see page 199, bottom).

Low-methoxyl (LM) pectin. Perhaps the trickiest to use, but the most flexible, is LM pectin. Its gelling ability relies on the addition of calcium powder, which comes with the pectin, so it will gel even in reduced- or no-sugar recipes. Mix the calcium powder with water in a ratio of ½ teaspoon powder to ½ cup water and set aside. Combine your sugar and pectin and set aside. Stir the calcium water into the cooked fruit, then sprinkle in the sugar-pectin mixture and stir to dissolve. For a no-sugar jam, measure 1 cup of cooked fruit and blend it with the pectin. Add the calcium water to the remaining cooked fruit, and then add the fruit-pectin mixture, stirring to dissolve. (See more on page 196.)

Liquid pectin. Liquid pectin has a short shelf life, so you need to buy new each season. The open packages also do not keep. To use it, cook your fruit, add the sugar, bring to a boil, and then add the pectin.

Powdered pectin. Like liquid pectin, commercial powdered pectin loses strength with age. Buy fresh pectin each season. Opened packages can be used if resealed tightly. To get a gel with powdered pectin, cook your fruit, add the pectin, and return to a boil. Then add your sugar and boil again to dissolve.

Q Can I substitute powdered pectin for liquid?

A No, you can't swap one kind of pectin for another. You have to follow your recipe as indicated. Different pectins are treated differently in the pot.

PEEL-AND-PIP PECTIN

Makes about 1 quart

What did cooks do before they had pectin in a box? They made their own. It's not difficult to do, and the texture homemade pectin brings to your jams and jellies is ideal — silky and delicate. The pectin from this recipe looks like a syrupy liquid. It doesn't reach gel stage until it cooks up with your fruit.

INGREDIENTS

4   pounds underripe tart or crab apples, quartered, but not peeled or cored (or a combination of apples plus additional apple peels and cores)

1   quart water

¼   cup bottled lemon juice

PREPARE

1. Combine the apples, water, and lemon juice in a large nonreactive pot and bring to a boil. Reduce the heat and simmer for 1 hour, uncovered, stirring occasionally to prevent scorching.

2. Line a colander with a triple layer of cheesecloth or have ready a jelly bag in its frame, and set either device over a large pot or bowl. Gently pour the apple mixture into your straining setup. Allow the cooked fruit to drain for 3 to 4 hours, until all the juice has been released. (Do not press on the draining fruit; doing so will cloud the liquid.) Use immediately or preserve for later.

PRESERVE

Refrigerate: Ladle into bowls or jars. Cover and refrigerate for up to 5 days.

Freeze: Pectin can be frozen for up to 6 months. However, freezing will weaken the pectin slightly, so you will have to use about one-third more of it for the same gelling effect as refrigerated or canned pectin.

Can: Use the boiling-water method (see page 95). Wipe out your pot, return the strained juice to it, and bring it to a boil. Ladle the pectin into clean, hot half-pint canning jars, leaving ¼ inch of headspace. Use a bubble tool, or other nonmetallic implement, to release any trapped air. Wipe the rims, cover the jars, and screw the bands on just fingertip-tight. Process for 10 minutes. Cool for 24 hours. Check the seals and store in a cool, dark place for up to 1 year.

Q How do you use low-methoxyl (LM) pectin?

A Low-methoxyl pectins, such as Pomona's Universal Pectin, are easy to use, but they do act differently from the other commercial pectins available. Before you begin your recipe, you need to make calcium water by combining the calcium powder that comes in the kit with water. For the Pomona's Pectin, you combine ½ teaspoon of calcium powder with ½ cup water. Set this aside until you are ready to use it. You can store unused calcium water in the refrigerator, where it will keep, covered, for several months. You also need to combine the pectin with the sugar used in your recipe and set that mixture aside.

To add the pectin to your recipe:

1. Cook and mash your fruit until your desired texture is reached.

2. Stir in the amount of calcium water indicated in the recipe; then add the sugar-pectin mixture. Simmer for 1 to 2 minutes to dissolve the sugar and the pectin.

3. Remove from heat and let stand for 5 minutes, stirring occasionally, to allow any trapped air to settle out of your jam mixture. Skim off any foam, ladle your jam into your prepared jars, and process according to your recipe's instructions.

Q Why do you use low-methoxyl (LM) pectin?

A Low-methoxyl pectin, such as Pomona's Universal Pectin, allows greater versatility in your recipe. Here are some of the benefits of using LM pectin:

- Because LM pectins rely on calcium, included in the pectin kit, to gel rather than sugar, you can use much less sugar in your recipe.

- You can use alternative sweeteners such as honey or agave in your recipes and still get a good gel.

- LM pectins last longer on the shelf. No need to buy fresh product each canning season.

- LM pectins are free of additives; they are just pure pectin derived from citrus peels.

Sugar and Acid

Q The amount of sugar in jam recipes seems really excessive. Why so much?

A Yes, to those new to preserving, the amount of sugar in the recipes can seem a bit too much. But sugar isn't there just to be sweet. It has chemical properties that are very important to the process. Here's what sugar does:

- **Encourages gel.** Sugar acts with acid and pectin to create a thick texture.

- **Preserves color.** Sugar keeps sweet spreads looking bright on the shelf.

- **Adds glossy sheen.** Sugar gives spreads their sparkle.

- **Protects the texture of the fruit.** Sugar toughens the cell walls of fruit, helping to preserve its texture during the cooking and preserving process.

- **Extends shelf life.** While acid is the essential ingredient in safe canning, sugar does extend the shelf life of the spread once the jar is opened.

You can use less sugar, or even alternative sweeteners, but your results will be affected. Spreads may not be as thick; they may be dull on the spoon, fade in the jar, and expire quickly once opened.

Q My strawberries always fall apart during cooking. How do I get big pieces of fruit in my jam?

A The key to keeping the fruits in your spreads whole lies in the sugar and when it is added to the pot. Sugar toughens the cell walls of fruit, so you can use the timing of its entry into the recipe to avoid or take advantage of this property. Here are some tips on creating the texture you want:

- Cook your fruit down and then add the sugar last for a smooth-textured jam. Use this method whenever you want the produce to break down, such as when preparing a sauce or fruit leather.

- Add the sugar and fruit to the pot at the same time for a somewhat toothsome product.

- Combine the sugar and the fruit the night before your jam making. Macerating the fruit in this way gives the sugar a chance to toughen the cell walls of the fruit. The next day, the fruit will have given off a lot of juice and look quite deflated, but, because it has been subjected to sugar for so long, it will be better able to hold its shape once it hits the heat.

Q Why doesn't my homemade jam last as long in the fridge as store-bought jams?

A Read the label on store-bought jams. Often they list sugar as their first ingredient, along with additives and preservatives that keep commercially produced foods picture-perfect seemingly forever. High amounts of sugar, additives, and preservatives can all make commercially produced spreads last longer than those you make at home. Although this means that homemade spreads will spoil sooner, it in no way indicates that they are inferior to commercially produced items. In fact, it's just the opposite. One of the benefits of home food preservation is that you can control your ingredients. If you are trying to reduce the number of additives and artificial ingredients in your diet or if you are trying to reduce your sugar intake, preserving your own food is a great place to start.

Q Should I use light or dark brown sugar in my recipes?

A Most brown sugar is actually granulated white sugar that has been sprayed with a coating of molasses to give it its characteristic color and flavor. You can use either light or dark in your recipes that call for brown sugar, but keep in mind that the darker the sugar, the more pronounced the molasses flavor.

Q Can I use other sweeteners besides white sugar?

A Yes and no. Some home preservation processes, such as making classic jams and jellies, require sugar to get a good set. Without sugar, you won't get the proper jelled consistency.

Sugar also acts to preserve texture and color, so canned items made without it or with reduced amounts may dull in color or become too soft to be considered successful. This applies to sweet spreads and pickles as well.

That being said, eaters who prefer to limit their sugar intake often find the trade-off worthwhile and are willing to step away from what many would consider "perfect jam" if it means they can enjoy more of it. For such eaters, quick jams that use commercial pectin are the answer. Low-methoxyl (LM) pectin, which relies on calcium to gel rather than sugar, can be used in low- or even no-sugar spreads (see page 196). You can also use alternative sweeteners such as stevia, agave syrup, and honey with this kind of pectin.

Artificial sweeteners, such as aspartame and sucralose, often take on a bitter flavor when cooked and are not recommended.

Q Why do I have to use lemon juice in my jams and jellies?

A When you are making your own preserves, lemon juice serves two purposes. First, it guarantees that you have the proper acidic pH for your food to stay safe on the shelf. Second, the acid works with the pectin in your recipe to help the preserves set into the thick, gelled texture that you seek.

Q Can I use any other acid in my fruit spread recipes?

A Technically, you could add other acids such as vinegar to your sweet spread recipes. The acid would perform the same job as lemon juice, encouraging a good set. However, the vinegar will alter the spread's flavor. This can be desirable in savory spreads such as tomato or chile pepper jam. However, vinegar can taste out of place in many fruit spreads. Follow your recipe for best results.

Getting a Good Set

Q How do I know when I've reached the gel stage?

A There are three tests that you can do to determine if your long-cooking jam has reached the gel stage:

- **Temperature.** Jams gel at 220°F. It seems quite simple — cook the jam until it hits the magic number and then pull it off the heat. But it's not always that straightforward. Jam making isn't just science; it is also an art. Use that 220 number as your guide and then back it up with the two tests that follow.

- **Sheeting.** If you've never seen sheeting, it's hard to picture. But once you get the hang of it, looking for jam to sheet will be a handy tool for telling whether you have reached that magical gel stage. It's essentially when two drops become one, a marriage if you will, of drips off the spoon. Here's how it works: Stir your almost-done jam with a wooden spoon. Lift the spoon sideways from the pot. In a too-thin jam, the drops will stream off the bottom edge of the spoon. As you get closer to the gel stage, the hot jam will drip. When you have reached the gel stage, the drops will join, forming a sheet, before falling into the pot.

sheeting

- **Wrinkle test.** This is my favorite test. It is the easiest and the one that I find the most reliable. The test is done like this: Put a clean plate in the freezer to chill while you're preparing the recipe. When you have sheeting, dribble a few drops of hot jam onto the plate's cold surface, give it a minute to cool, and then push on the little spot of jam with your finger, like you are trying to wipe it off. If the smudge of jam wrinkles when you start to push against it, the jam is ready. If it is thick but does not wrinkle, you need to cook it a bit more. (And if you are like me and forget to freeze your plate, just dribble the jam on the bottom of an ice cream carton to do the wrinkle test.)

wrinkle test

Q My grandmother never used added pectin in her jams. How did she get them to set?

A Oh, grannies. They have all the secrets! There are a few ways that your gran, or you, can get a jam to set without adding commercial pectin.

- Start with high-pectin fruit. Fruits such as cranberries have enough of their own naturally occurring pectin to set up easily when combined with sugar and acid.

- Add some high-pectin fruit, such as apples, to your mixture. Apples have a neutral flavor when cooked that combines easily with other fruits such as berries. They will boost your gel without interfering with the taste.

- Underripe fruit has more pectin than fully ripe produce. Include 20 to 25 percent slightly underripe fruit in your batch to ensure a good gel.

- Avoid overripened fruits. Pectin levels decrease as the fruit ripens. It's hard to get soft fruits to gel properly.

- The peels and pips from apples and citrus fruits are high in pectin. Tie them in a single piece of cheesecloth and boil them along with your fruit to boost your preserve's ability to gel.

- Make your own pectin, which is not as difficult as it sounds. Extract the pectin stock from fruits such as apples and you can have a natural source of pectin on hand (page 194).

Q Can I double or triple my batch?

A I don't recommend increasing the volume of your recipe when canning. Recipes for home food preservation are developed very precisely to give you consistent, reliable results. Of course there will be some variation with yields and cooking times depending on the power of your cooktop and the kind and size of the pots that you use, but increasing the amount of food called for in your recipe, even if you keep the proportions the same, can throw things very widely off. It can be hard to get a good set for things like jams and jellies, and large batches can easily scorch on the bottom before they are even warm on the surface. If you want to make a large batch of a recipe, find one that is developed for big-batch processing. Or, do successive small batches for tasty results you can trust.

Q How can I keep my jam from separating into fruit on the top and clear jelly on the bottom?

A You are experiencing the dreaded *fruit float*. It occurs when the air present in the cell walls of the produce hasn't cooked out because the food has been lightly cooked or not cooked at all. This trapped air causes the fruit to bob to the top of the canning jars during processing. Fruit float often settles out over time in whole fruits but is very noticeable in jams, where the gelled texture prevents the fruit from redistributing over time. Here are a few ways to avoid it in your spreads:

- Cutting or mashing fruit or cooking it for an extended period of time is a good way to minimize fruit float. The mechanical process physically breaks the cell walls of the fruit, releasing the air that is trapped in them.

- Avoid overripe fruit, which tends to float more than just-right fruit.

- It is also most beneficial to cool your jam, just slightly, before ladling it into your jars; this gives the jam a chance to thicken to a point that will better suspend the fruit. Giving your jam a good stir for 5 minutes after you take it off the heat ought to do it.

- If you still have fruit float, you can flip your jars temporarily to give the fruit a chance to redistribute before the preserves set into their gelled texture. Wait until the seals have begun to form but the jam is still warm in the jars — 1½ to 2 hours after you remove them from the boiling water — and then invert them until cooled. Return the jars to their upright position for long-term storage.

Q Why is my jam so stiff?

A The most common cause of stiff jam is overcooking. While no one wants a thin jam, it's better to err on the side of thin rather than overcooked. So, when in doubt, it's better to undercook than overcook. A thin spread can be used as a syrup — pour it over pancakes or ice cream, or add it to a vinaigrette or a pan sauce for a blast of fruity flavor. But a too-thick spread is tarry and unpleasant to eat. Stiff spreads can be remade by thinning them with a bit of water, bringing the mixture briefly to a boil, and then reprocessing in clean, hot jars.

Q Does altitude affect my jelly making?

A Yes, making sweet spreads at higher elevations does take some special consideration. Because the boiling point is lower, it can take these spreads longer to reach the gel stage, causing increased evaporation in the pot and a stiff jam.

Because liquids boil at lower temperatures in higher elevations, the gel temperature (220°F at sea level) will not be accurate. You can try to adjust for altitude, lowering the target temperature 2°F for every 1,000 feet above sea level, or rely on the sheeting or wrinkle test to know when you have a good set.

Q My jam didn't set. Is there anything I can do?

A Even the most experienced canner will sometimes cook up a pot of jam that just doesn't gel correctly. You can simply enjoy it as a fruit sauce, or return it to the pot, bring to a simmer, and try one of the following remedies:

- **Give it a bit more time.** If you are cooking up a classic spread — one that doesn't use added pectin — you can try to cook it a little longer, stirring all the while, to see if you get a better gel.

- **Add a little more acid.** Acid helps pectin set, so add another tablespoon or so of bottled lemon juice to the mix, stir for a few minutes, and see if it comes together.

- **Add a bit of commercial pectin.** If you are using Pomona's Universal Pectin, which is the most versatile, add 1 teaspoon of the calcium water to the pot, then add ¼ cup of sugar blended with 1 teaspoon of pectin. Stir for 1 to 2 minutes to dissolve the sugar. You can then refill your jars and process again.

Troubleshooting

Q My friends and I made a huge pot of blueberry jam and it didn't set. What happened?

A I am going to run with the clue you've given me here. It is very hard to get a *huge* pot of jam to gel. There is just too much volume to get a uniform temperature throughout the mixture. By the time the jam in the middle is done, that on the bottom is scorched and that on the top is not ready yet — even with constant stirring, it's hard to get a consistent result in a very large vessel. To get the best results, cook multiple small batches rather than one large pot. The texture will be easier to control. Also, the less time the pan stays on the heat, the fruitier the preserves will taste.

Q My grandmother used to just scrape the mold off the top of her jam when she opened the jars. Is it safe to eat moldy jam?

A It's true: home preservers of years past used to peel off any mold they found on top of their preserves and dig right in. Some still do. It used to be believed that the mold was harmless, but that has since been proven untrue. The mold that you see is just the tip of the iceberg, so to speak. Visible mold is just the cap of a colony of spores that reaches down into the jar. You can remove the mold cap, but that doesn't mean that you will be removing the tendrils that reach down into the jam, and those spores can sicken you. Mold is a sign of spoilage. If you see any on the top of your food or inside the lid of your jar, discard promptly.

Q Why is my jelly cloudy?

A Cloudy jelly is most often the result of a misstep during the juicing process. For crystal-clear jelly, follow these tips:

- Cook fruit gently. Boiling the fruit will cloud the juice.

- Strain slowly. Hang your fruit in the finest mesh jelly bag or multiple layers of cheesecloth to strain out even the finest fruit particles.

- Don't squeeze! It's so tempting to squeeze the jelly bag to nudge the process along or get the last bit of juice out of the fruit, but doing so will force fruit particles through the mesh.

If your jelly looks a little less than crystal clear coming out of the canner, don't fret. It will still taste great. Cloudiness that develops during storage, however, is a sign of spoilage. Discard immediately!

Q Why are there bubbles in my jelly?

A Bubbles in jelly can be caused by two things. If the bubbles are moving, the jelly is fermenting. Discard this immediately, as it is spoiled and cannot be remade. Chances are that the jelly was not processed long enough to destroy bacteria.

If the bubbles show no movement, then they are just air trapped in suspension. It's important to ladle the jelly into the jar while it is still hot. Jelly that has begun to set is likely to trap air as it finishes its set. Ladle the jelly into the jars gently. When jelly is poured from too high of a distance, it splashes into the jar with air in it from the agitation that may not be able to escape before the spread sets.

Q What could make my jam taste bitter?

A Bitter jam is most likely the result of overcooking the recipe. If you cook at too high a heat or do not stir often enough, you can scorch your jam. The color will darken and the jam can take on a bitter flavor.

Q Why is there a little puddle of liquid on the top of my jam?

A Pooling liquid on top of jam or jelly, also called weeping, can be caused by excessive acid in your recipe or by storing your preserves in a location that is very warm. Always follow your recipe and try to store preserves in a cool, dry place.

Q My jam is fizzing. Can I still eat it?

A Please don't. Carbonation is one of the telltale signs of fermentation. You can expect to see these tiny bubbles in your kraut as it sours as a natural part of the aerobic fermentation process. Fermentation in the anaerobic environment of a sealed jar means that either the seal has been compromised or the food is not acidic enough to remain stable. Any bubbles that are moving through the jar are a clear indication that something is wrong. Carefully dispose of the food so that no human or animal will accidentally ingest it. Be sure to sterilize the jars before reusing them to prevent any bacteria from infecting your next batch of preserves. To do it, just wash the jars with hot, soapy water and submerge the clean jars in boiling water for 10 minutes.

Q What would make my grape jelly have a gritty texture?

A Grape juice can sometimes form tartrate crystals, which interfere with a smooth-textured jam. To avoid these crystals, allow the juice for jelly to settle overnight in the refrigerator. Carefully pour off the juice, leaving the crystals behind, or strain it through a double thickness of cheesecloth before proceeding with your recipe.

Q Why does my jam have sugar crystals in it?

A No one wants a gritty texture in their spread. Sugar crystals can be caused by not fully dissolving the sugar. Always run a wooden spoon along the bottom of the jelly pan to feel for the sand of undissolved crystals. You want to ensure that all sugar and pectin are fully dissolved.

Sugar crystals may also be caused by using too much sugar, creating a supersaturated solution that will recrystallize as it cools. You can avoid this by following your recipe precisely and never adding more sugar than is called for or overcooking your spread, which will concentrate the sugar in the recipe and cause crystals to form.

Q My jam's color appears to have faded. Is there anything I can do to set the color?

A The colors of preserves can fade a bit over time, particularly in low-sugar jams. The best way to prevent any dulling is to use all of the sugar indicated in the recipe. Keep the filled jars stored in a cool place away from direct sunlight, which can cause fading in its own right.

Q What is the best way to skim foam? I feel like I lose half my jam!

A When you take the jam off the heat, let it rest for 5 minutes, stirring occasionally so that all of the bubbles rise to the top before you start skimming. Then use your ladle to lightly brush over the surface of the jam, sort of corralling all of the bubbles over to the side of the pot. Then you can skim them off in one or two scoops. Some people use a pat of butter in the pot to reduce foaming, but that's not good for vegan friends, and it can grease up the rim, making it harder to get a good seal. (See more on page 184.)

CHAPTER 13

Pickles

Every culture seems to have its own pickle tradition, from Eastern European fermented half-sours to Indian chutneys and Asian fish sauces. Pickles perk up the plate and are said to aid digestion. That's why it is common to find a pickle garnishing a heavy or spicy meal. The kosher dill alongside your deli sandwich isn't just a snack; it's a pairing that supposedly helps the body deal with that double pastrami on rye. Whether you enjoy your pickles for their taste or for their medicinal benefits, they are a great addition to the plate. Here is some more info on how to make your pickles perfection.

Q **What is the difference between a vinegar pickle and a fermented pickle?**

A All pickles require acid for safe storage. Vinegar pickles, sometimes called quick pickles, get their acidification from (you guessed it) vinegar. Fermented pickles get their acidification from lactic acid, which forms during the fermentation process. Both pickles will have the sour, pungent taste that the acid brings. However, the fermented pickles have a bit more subtlety to their flavor and offer the added bonus of being loaded with probiotics, the beneficial bacteria that convert the produce's sugars to acid during the fermentation process.

Q **Do I have to use salt in my vinegar pickles?**

A Unlike fermented pickles, which rely on precise amounts of salt to abate contaminants, vinegar pickles use salt for flavoring alone. If you are on a low-salt diet, you can certainly leave the salt out of your vinegar pickle recipe, or add a bit more, if that's to your liking.

Q **What is pickling spice? Can I use a substitute?**

A Pickling spice is nothing more than a combination of dried spices that you would typically find in pickle brine. Most commonly it contains mustard seeds, celery seeds, pepper, and maybe a bit of clove or allspice. You can certainly make one of your own, customizing it with the flavors that you like best. Try the recipe on the following page to get you started, but feel free to improvise.

PICKLING SPICE

Makes about ¾ cup

*You don't need to purchase a task-specific spice for pickling —
just whip up a batch of this mix from your spice rack. You can
also try taking out the mustard, celery, and dill and adding
cumin, coriander, and turmeric for an Indian-flavored spice
mix; or throw in some juniper berries if you have them on hand,
kick up the heat with a variety of peppercorns, or add some dried
ginger and cinnamon to warm up the tone of the blend. The best
pickling spice is your pickling spice.*

INGREDIENTS

2 dried California or 5 Turkish bay leaves, crushed

¼ cup yellow mustard seeds

2 tablespoons celery seeds

1 tablespoon allspice berries

2 tablespoons black peppercorns

2 tablespoons dill seeds

1 teaspoon whole cloves

PREPARE

Combine the bay leaves, mustard seeds, celery seeds, allspice,
peppercorns, dill seeds, and cloves in a small, airtight jar. Keep
in a cool, dark place for up to 1 year.

Q I want to pickle chile peppers. Should I use the hot-pack or cold-pack method?

A Pickled chiles are a treat to have on hand. They are terrific added to eggs, strewn on a pizza, or tucked into a sandwich. And the spicy pickling liquid is a tangy, tasty hot sauce all on its own.

I once made the mistake of trying to hot pack my chiles. Let me tell you, the minute the peppers hit the hot brine, my whole kitchen was filled with chile-spiked steam. Even my dog's eyes were watering. Makes sense: pepper spray is made from capsaicin, the compound in peppers that gives them their heat and their eye-stinging vengeance if it becomes airborne.

Don't let this happen to you! Use the cold-pack method for chiles. Press your prepared peppers into clean, hot jars. Pour your hot brine over them and then prepare your jars for the canner. That way, all of that great chile kick stays in the jar where it belongs.

Q Why do I need to salt and drain my produce before pickling it?

A Salting draws excess moisture out of produce. This will make the pickles crisper. Also, and most important, it draws out the extra water in the produce that can dilute your brine and jeopardize your results. So it's an important step and easy to do:

1. Toss your prepared foods with the amount of salt indicated in your recipe; some recipes call for topping the salted produce with ice, a step that further crisps the produce and keeps it chilled before processing.

2. After the recommended waiting time, rinse your produce thoroughly to remove the excess salt.

3. Drain thoroughly to be sure that any excess moisture is left behind. It is not necessary, however, to towel-dry or air-dry food before proceeding with your recipe. Just a good soak and draining will remove all of the liquid necessary for a good pickle.

Q Why is my pickled garlic blue? Is it still safe to eat?

A Garlic that turns blue during pickling may be shocking to look at but will taste no different from cloves that maintain their creamy white hue in the jar. Blue cloves are just as safe to eat as those that haven't discolored.

The blue tone is a reaction of the anthocyanins, water-soluble pigments in the cloves of garlic, with the acids in the brine. The color change can be more pronounced in immature garlic, but it varies greatly from head to head and even among cloves in the same head.

Q My chutney is cloudy. Can I still eat it?

A Ground spices can often cause preparations such as chutneys to appear cloudy in the jar. Turmeric, an ingredient frequently used in chutney recipes, is a common culprit. But any ground spice can cause this clouding. It isn't harmful and is hard to avoid when using ground spices, which will muddy a brine just like a bit of silt in a puddle of water.

When possible, opt for whole spices in your preserves to avoid any clouding. They act more like pebbles in the puddle — you can see them, but the water they are in remains clear.

Clouding that occurs in the absence of ground spices may be a sign of deterioration. Always inspect your canned food thoroughly before serving. When in doubt, throw it out.

Kitchen Tip

When using ground or powdered spices, it's best to start with whole spices and grind them as needed for the freshest flavor and to avoid any musty taste in your products.

Q My recipe didn't make enough brine to cover my cucumbers. Do I have to start all over?

A It is imperative that all produce be completely submerged under brine for successful pickle making. You don't have to start all over, but you do need to top up your jars before processing. The easiest way to do this is to quickly bring a small amount of brine to a boil and add it to your jars. You don't have to use the same amounts indicated in your recipe, or even include the spices indicated, but you do need to use the same proportions of vinegar to water. When in doubt, always err on the side of a more acidic brine — one with a greater proportion of vinegar to water — than a weak one.

And always make sure that you boil your brine before adding it to your jars or it will cool the contents of your jar and throw off your processing time.

Q How long do I have to wait before I can eat my canned pickles and relishes?

A You can eat them as soon as they are cool, but pickles and relishes benefit from a bit of time on the shelf. I give mine 3 to 4 weeks before I dive in to allow the flavors to blend and mellow a bit and for the brines to fully penetrate the produce.

Q Can I cook my brine down to concentrate its flavors?

A Never cook your brine for longer than indicated in the recipe. Vinegar loses acidity as it cooks. Extended boiling can change the pH of the brine, jeopardizing your results.

Q Do I have to use Kirby cucumbers to make pickles? Are other varieties suitable?

A Kirby cucumbers have a thin skin that is less bitter than that of slicing cucumbers and have relatively few seeds, making them a good candidate for pickling. But you can use any low-seed variety, such as lemon cucumbers and gherkins. And, in all honesty, when the cukes start coming, I throw whatever I have into the brine. It all tastes pretty good!

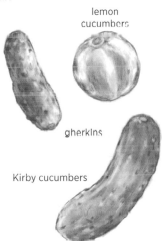

lemon cucumbers

gherkins

Kirby cucumbers

Q I've eaten all of my vinegar pickles. Is there any use for the leftover brine?

A Oh, I love a good leftovers recipe. And the brine from vinegar pickles is a key ingredient in some real gems. A very dear friend and avid pickler, Luke Easter, gave me this tip for using up the spices at the bottom of the pickle jar — which often is made up of a fair amount of mustard seeds: strain the spices out of the brine and grind them into a paste for a quick homemade mustard. You can also blend the mustard with a little mayonnaise and olive oil for an easy sandwich spread.

Some pickle lovers enjoy their brine so much that they drink it, cocktail style. A shot of Jameson Irish Whisky followed by a shot of pickle juice (pick your flavor) is known as a pickleback and is growing in popularity.

Q I accidentally left the salt out of the brine in my bread and butter chips. Is that okay?

A Salt is used exclusively as a flavoring in the brine of vinegar pickles. Salt can help to toughen the cell walls, essentially crisping the vegetable prior to processing. But the only time it is related to safety is in the fermentation process, which uses salt to create an environment that is inhospitable to contaminating pathogens.

If you realize that you left the salt out of your recipe before you seal your jars, you can just add a small amount to each jar. If it doesn't occur to you until after the jars come out of the canner, then you might just add a bit when you open each jar. The flavor won't be the same, but chances are, the salt used to initially soak the cucumbers will bring enough flavor to the table to save the day.

Q All of this vinegar makes my pickles so sour. Can I use less for a sweeter pickle?

A Absolutely *never* reduce the amount of vinegar listed in your recipe. It is the vinegar in the recipe that makes the processed pickles acidic enough to safely store on your shelf. Lessening the amount of vinegar can reduce the pH of your recipe to a dangerous level. If you would like a sweeter pickle, you can add a bit more sugar to take the bite out of the vinegar. Keep in mind, however, that the flavor of vinegar pickles will mellow after some time on the shelf. The pickle that tastes pungent in the pot might be perfect after a few weeks in the sealed jar.

CHAPTER 14

Sauces

Condiments and sauces can make the meal: a great barbecue sauce to mop on grilled foods, a dipping sauce for dunking tasty finger foods, sweet sauces to drizzle on dessert. Having a few preserved sauces in your pantry or freezer can throw a basic dinner over the top, turning something *blah* into something *ah!* Make your sauces super with these tips and tricks.

Q How can I tell when my applesauce is fully cooked?

A Applesauce thickness is really a matter of preference; some like it thicker than others. The only thing you don't want is watery applesauce. To avoid that, do this test. Scoop out a spoonful of sauce onto a plate or saucer. If a ring of liquid forms around the dollop of applesauce, it's not quite done. Keep cooking until it no longer weeps. If you prefer a very thick sauce, you can keep cooking for quite a long time — all the way to apple butter, which is really just applesauce that has been cooked for an extended period of time.

weeping applesauce

Q I made a recipe for strawberry sauce and it's so thin that it looks like strawberry juice.

A Fruit sauces, such as strawberry and blueberry sauce, will often thicken during storage. Give them a few weeks on the shelf for the pectin to firm up and you will have a thick but pourable sauce. If you cook your sauce to a point where it is thick right off the stove, it will be too firm by the time it cools and sets up on the shelf.

Q I have seen a lot of recipes for fruit ketchups. What makes these sauces ketchups?

A We think of ketchup as a tomato-based spread, but it didn't start out that way. Ketchup originated, like many foods such as spaghetti, in China, where it was known as *kachiap*, a common

BLUEBERRY GASTRIQUE

Makes about 1½ cups

I can't get enough of this sensational sauce. It's easy, versatile, and delicious! The name may make it sound complicated but it is really so simple to make — and quite fun, too. The technique of making the caramel base is a basic kitchen skill you can use to create a lot of great recipes, like the sauce for flan, a butterscotch pudding, even lollipops, so it's a useful one to have in your cooking repertoire — and it's quite fascinating to witness, too. (Yes, I am a bit of a science geek.)

INGREDIENTS

    1 cup sugar
    ¼ cup water
    1 cup red wine vinegar
    2 cups (about ¾ pound) berries
       Pinch of salt

PREPARE

1. Combine the sugar and water in a medium saucepan. Bring to a light boil over medium-low heat. Do not stir. Cook until the sugar melts and begins to color slightly, 5 to 7 minutes, washing down the sides of the pan with a pastry brush as necessary. Pour the vinegar into the pan, but be careful — the vinegar will hiss and spit a good bit. The caramel will harden when the liquid hits it but will dissolve in the vinegar as it simmers. Simmer until reduced by half, about 5 minutes.

2. Add the berries and continue to simmer until the sauce takes on the color and fragrance of the fruit and thickens slightly, about 10 minutes. Strain through a fine-mesh sieve. Finish with a sprinkle of salt.

PRESERVE

Refrigerate: Ladle into bowls or jars. The gastrique will keep, covered, for up to 3 weeks.

Freeze: Freeze the gastrique in a covered ice cube tray or small containers for up to 6 months.

Can: Use the boiling-water method (see page 95). Ladle the gastrique into clean, hot 4-ounce jars. Use a bubble tool, or other nonmetallic implement, to release any trapped air. Wipe the rims, cover the jars, and screw the bands on just fingertip-tight. Process for 10 minutes. Cool for 24 hours. Check the seals and store in a cool, dark place for up to 1 year.

table condiment made out of pickled fish and spices. Kachiap was eventually discovered by English colonialists, who put their own distinct spin on the original Chinese name and recipe, calling it *ketchup* and incorporating nuts and mushrooms into the formula. When the condiment reached American shores, it again morphed as all kinds of produce, including rhubarb, became the base of the sauce. It wasn't until 1876, when the H. J. Heinz Company featured a tomato ketchup in its product line, that the now-popular version became the standard. So really, you would have to pick your moment in food history to find a specific recipe for ketchup.

Q What's the difference between applesauce and apple butter?

A Apple butter is just applesauce that has been cooked a bit longer for a thicker, spreadable consistency. Other fruit butters, such as peach butter, work the same way. Chopped fruit is cooked until soft and puréed. The purée is cooked down to a sauce and then further cooked to achieve its signature consistency. Butters require careful attention in the pot, with near constant stirring at the end of the process, as their thick texture can cause them to burn quite easily.

Q My barbecue sauce has a thin band of water at the bottom of the jar. Is that okay?

A You may see a thin band of water or clear liquid at the bottom of a processed jar of sauce. This is not harmful and can be caused by a couple different things. Your pectin may have separated from your sauce. This sometimes happens when a sauce is cooked for too long and the pectin breaks. It may cause your sauce to be a little less thick, but it has no impact on safety. To avoid broken pectin in the future, avoid overcooking your sauce.

You may also be experiencing something like fruit float. The solids of your mixture have separated out of the suspension during processing, leaving a bit of liquid at the bottom of the jar. To avoid this in the future, allow your sauce to cool for a few minutes — no longer than 5 — stirring occasionally to give the sauce a chance to thicken before being ladled into the jars.

In either case, it wouldn't hurt to shake the jar a bit after it has cooled to redistribute the contents. Or you can just remix before serving.

CHAPTER 15

Vegetables

There are lots of ways to use up the bounty of the harvest season. Vegetables can be used in both savory and sweet recipes. They can be turned into pickles, jams, relishes, and chutneys. Pressure canned or frozen, they can provide a supply of locally grown foods all year round. Root cellars are terrific for stowing away fall keepers, such as apples, root vegetables, hardy cabbages, and more. Many vegetables can be dried and stored in a fraction of the space. Take good care of your vegetables and they'll take good care of you!

Q My father sent me a 25-pound bag of Vidalia onions. What's the best way to preserve them?

A Sweet onions, such as Vidalia and Walla Walla, are a treat. It's great to enjoy them when they come into season. Their delicate flavor is matched, however, by a shorter shelf life than regular yellow storage onions, so it's a good idea to have a plan for those that won't be eaten right away. Here are a few ideas:

- **Root cellar.** You can store sweet onions for a short time in a cool basement. You will get the longest storage time out of them if you provide good air circulation around them. One way to do this is to drop them down into the leg of an old pair of panty hose or tights, knotting between each onion so that they don't touch each other. Weird looking, but effective.

- **Pickle.** You can prepare sweet onions like other hot-packed pickles. Bring them to a boil in a brine, pack them into jars, and use the boiling-water method (see page 95) to can them.

- **Freeze.** My favorite way to store the onions is to chop them, sprinkle with a little salt, and cook them way down with a good amount of butter over medium-low heat in a Dutch oven or heavy-bottomed pan until brown and jammy. Transfer the cooled, caramelized onions to freezer-proof containers and freeze for up to 6 months. You can do 5 pounds at a time this way.

Q The bottled roasted red peppers sold in the store are so expensive. How can I make my own?

A Roasted peppers and chiles are so versatile, and it is great to have them on hand. Strewn on pizzas, stuffed into sandwiches, or whirred into blended soups, dips, and dressings — the list of uses has no end. There are several ways to prepare them and a few ways to preserve them.

1. First, you need to char your peppers or chiles, making sure the skin is completely black. There are several ways to do this; rub them lightly with oil, then do any of the following:

   - Run them under your oven broiler, several inches from the element.

   - Char them on your outdoor grill.

   - Hold them (with heatproof tongs) directly over the flame of your gas burner.

2. Place the peppers in a heatproof bowl or pan and cover tightly for 5 minutes to loosen the skins.

3. When the peppers are cool enough to handle, gently slip the charred skins, seeds, and ribs from the flesh.

4. Now you're ready to preserve the roasted peppers:

- **Freezing:** Be sure to pack them in small containers so that you have to defrost only the amount you need.

- **Pressure canning:** Divide them into clean half-pint jars, top with boiling water, and process for 35 minutes at 11 psi if you are using a dial-gauge canner, 10 psi for a weighted-gauge canner.

- *Never* **use the boiling-water method to can peppers in water** — there is not sufficient acid present to do so safely.

Q I love to have chopped garlic on hand. What's the best way to keep it around?

A Having prepared garlic on hand is handy indeed. Unlike commercially prepared garlic, which is treated with chemicals to preserve its shelf life, garlic that you chop at home must be properly stored to remain a wholesome product. For the best results, you can purée garlic with a small amount of oil and keep it in the refrigerator for 2 to 3 days. For longer storage, divide the purée in the compartments of an ice cube tray, cover, and freeze. You can then pop out a cube of purée whenever you need it without the risk of spoilage. Never store chopped or minced garlic, in oil or not, on your counter! Such garlic is a common cause of food contamination. Always refrigerate or freeze prepared garlic.

Q I canned some peppers in just water and they look fine. Can I eat them?

A Vegetables are low-acid foods that must be canned in a pressure canner or pickled with acid, such as vinegar. Canning them using the boiling-water method will not raise the temperature high enough to destroy any potential pathogens.

Just because your peppers look fine does not mean that all is well. Contamination can be odorless, colorless, and flavorless. Always follow your canning directions exactly and never deviate from the prescribed methods. Doing so can lead to very bad results.

Q I always wind up pitching half of my fresh herbs in the compost. How can I use them up before they go to waste?

A I am so guilty of this. You bring home a bunch of herbs — maybe a bouquet of cilantro, dill, parsley, or basil — use a bit that night and then remember the rest only when you find them, sad and slimy, lurking in the back of the fridge. Well, no more. Here's how to get the most out of your tasty sprigs.

- When you bring them home, trim off the bottoms as you would fresh flowers and, just like a bouquet, plunk them down into a container of water. Wrap the tops loosely with a bag or dampened paper towel and put the whole bouquet in the fridge. Use within 3 to 5 days. (Except basil, which will blacken in the chill of the fridge, so leave that bouquet on the counter.)

- If you see them start to get wilty, or you know that you just won't get through the bunch, you can purée them with a bit of water or oil, ladle the purée into an ice cube tray, and freeze into herb pops. Cover the tray or transfer the cubes to an airtight container or bag and they will keep in the freezer for 6 months.

- If you don't want to take up space in your freezer, arrange them in a single layer on a cookie sheet and dry in a low oven (170°F tops) until they are brittle. Crumble and store in airtight jars for up to 3 months.

Q Can green and red cabbage be used interchangeably?

A From a safety standpoint? Absolutely. And flavor-wise? Sure, red cabbage will taste great. Just keep in mind that your recipe — whatever it is — will be blasted with purple. It makes for lovely sauerkraut but might be a little garish in a relish, where the cabbage will color all of the ingredients with its neon hue.

Q Are there any vegetables that I can't can?

A Some vegetables, such as pumpkins and winter squash, have a dense, starchy texture that makes it hard to safely process them in a home kitchen. If you are going to take this project on, you must be very careful that you can only cubed squash flesh and that you use a pressure canner. Never can puréed or mashed pumpkin or winter squash — it is just too dense to get a safe result.

CHAPTER 16

Whole Fruits

The fruit season is so short. It makes sense to want to squirrel some away until the next year, like having time capsules of summer lined up on the shelf. It's easy to enjoy the way the jars look, but most of all, you are going to love the way the fruit tastes. Use these suggestions to get the most from your bounty.

Q I love canned peaches but not the thick syrup they often come packed in. Can you recommend a lighter alternative?

A Contrary to popular opinion, it is not the sugar that preserves the fruit; it's the acid. So, as long as you use any acidifying agents suggested in your recipe, you can use a lighter syrup for your preserving and still be safe. However, sugar does help protect the color and texture of the fruit, so fruits preserved in thin syrups may dull or soften more quickly than those preserved in sweeter solutions. The following chart offers some ratios of sugar to water that you can use to make a variety of syrups.

Syrup Preparations - Pressure Can (Nonacidic)	
Syrup consistency	**Sugar per 1 cup water**
Very light	2 tablespoons
Light	$1/4$ cup
Medium	$1/2$ cup
Heavy	$3/4$ cup
Very heavy	1 cup

Q Can I use honey to preserve my fruit instead of sugar?

A You can use honey in your syrups with delicious results. (See Pears in Honey Syrup, page 222.) However, some strongly flavored honeys, such as buckwheat honey, can overpower the taste of the fruit if used in large quantities. Sugar protects the flavor and color of the fruit in a way that honey does not, so that's something to take into consideration as well. Just as reduced-sugar fruits and

PEARS IN HONEY SYRUP

Makes about 4 quarts

Pears and honey are a fantastic combination. Use lighter variet-
ies of honey to support the flavor of the pears without overwhelm-
ing their own natural perfume or discoloring the fruit. When
choosing your pears, opt for firm fruit that will hold its shape
during this process. You can spice the syrup by adding a few star
anise, cinnamon sticks, or cloves to the pot. Remove them before
ladling over the pears, as their flavor will strengthen during stor-
age. In this recipe, you'll be creating an anti-browning, ascorbic
acid bath using crushed vitamin C tablets.

INGREDIENTS

6 (500 mg) vitamin C tablets, crushed

2 quarts plus 6 cups cold water

6 pounds pears

1 cup sugar

1 cup local honey
(preferably a light variety)

1 cup bottled lemon juice

PREPARE

1. In a large bowl, cooler, or your impeccably clean kitchen sink, dissolve the crushed vitamin C tablets in the 2 quarts of cold water.

2. Using a small paring knife, peel and halve the pears. Remove the cores with a melon baller or small spoon. Drop the pear halves into the acid bath as you go.

3. Bring the 6 cups of water, sugar, honey, and lemon juice to a boil in a medium saucepan, stirring to dissolve the sugar and honey. Scoop the pears from the acid bath and drain. Add the fruit to the boiling syrup and simmer for 5 minutes.

4. Pack the pears gently but firmly into four clean, hot quart jars. Ladle hot syrup over the pears to cover by ½ inch, leaving ½ inch of headspace between the top of the liquid and the lid. Screw the lids on the jars temporarily. Gently swirl the jars to release trapped air bubbles. Remove the lids and add syrup, if necessary, to achieve proper headspace.

PRESERVE

Can: Use the boiling-water method (see page 95). Wipe the rims, cover the jars, and screw the bands on just fingertip-tight. Process for 25 minutes. Turn off the heat, remove the canner lid, and let the jars rest in the water for 5 minutes. Remove the jars and set aside for 24 hours. Check seals, then store in a cool, dark place for up to 1 year.

spreads will dull and soften more quickly than their high-sugar counterparts, so will those that use honey rather than white sugar in their syrup.

To enjoy the flavor of honey without overwhelming the fruit and still reap the benefits of sugar, substitute half of the sugar with honey in light, medium, and heavy syrup preparations. Keep in mind that the amount of honey in your recipe can dramatically affect the flavor. In a very light syrup, the small amount of honey that would be used may not be enough to impart any discernable honey flavor to the recipe, unless you are using a very strongly flavored honey. The large amount of honey in a very heavy syrup may be too strong for your taste if you aren't working with a very lightly flavored honey.

Q Is there a way to can fruit without any added syrup?

A Yes, you may can fruit in water or fruit juice. Unsweetened apple or white grape juices are good choices. Because sugar protects color and texture, fruits canned without it will dull and soften more readily.

Fruits canned with water or fruit juice must be hot packed. Gently simmer fruits in water or juice until heated through. Ladle into jars, top with hot water or juice, and process as directed in your recipe.

Q How can I keep my whole fruits from bobbing to the top of the jar?

A All produce (all plants, for that matter) have oxygen stored in their cell structure. This trapped air makes uncooked fruits float to the top of your jar after processing. It's a condition (cleverly) called *fruit float*.

When canning whole fruits, the best way to avoid fruit float is to use the hot-pack method so that some of the air has a chance to cook out before the produce is packed in the jars. Also try to get as firm a pack as possible without crushing the fruit.

fruit float

Fruit float is not harmful and does not lead to spoilage. Often, the fruit will settle back down into the liquid after a bit of time on the shelf.

Q Do I need to peel plums before I can them?

A Tender-skinned fruits such as plums and apricots need not be peeled before canning. In fact, leaving the skins on these delicate fruits can help them keep their shape during processing.

Q I just processed some halved pears, and the fruits have tiny bubbles all over them. Are they safe to eat?

A A thin film of bubbles coating just-processed foods is harmless. Bubbles are formed by the air that is escaping from within the cell walls of the fruit. In a short time, they will rise to the top of the jar and become part of the headspace. However, bubbles rising from the fruit during storage — like Champagne on the side of a glass — are a sign of fermentation and indicate spoilage. Discard immediately!

Q What's the best way to remove air bubbles that are trapped in the divots of pitted, halved fruits?

A The divots of pitted fruits and the spaces between cold-packed fruits can trap a lot of air, and it's important to remove it. I find the best way to do it is to ladle your syrup or brine over the fruit, put the lid on, and gently swirl the liquid around from side to side so that it has a chance to fill these areas and force out the trapped air. You can then remove the lid, top off with more syrup or brine to reach the desired headspace, and proceed with processing.

Q I use cornstarch in my pie filling. Can I use that in my canned pie filling, too?

A Thickeners not specifically designed for canning are not recommended in the process. Cornstarch and wheat flour can separate out during the process, making for a less desirable result. Most important, these thickeners can make it difficult for heat to fully penetrate the jars, leaving your recipe underprocessed — a dangerous situation. Either use the special thickeners designed for canning or, better yet, can your pie filling without a thickener, and instead stir it into your fruit mixture before baking.

Q What's the difference between ascorbic acid and citric acid, and are they interchangeable?

A **Ascorbic acid,** also known as vitamin C, is used as an anti-browning agent. Crystals or tablets of it are dissolved in water to pretreat fruit, such as peaches and apples, that is likely to discolor during the preserving process.

Citric acid is used as an acidifying agent to lower the pH of recipes, such as those containing tomatoes, to a safe level for processing. It comes in powdered form and is added to the jars along with the food.

Lemon juice contains both ascorbic and citric acid.

Q Is it safe to can whole figs?

A Yes, although figs are a low-acid fruit, you may can them using the boiling-water method. You just need to acidify your syrup to do so safely. Add 2 tablespoons of bottled lemon juice or ½ teaspoon of citric acid per quart, or 1 tablespoon of lemon juice or ¼ teaspoon of citric acid per pint, to the jars of packed figs before ladling in your syrup.

CHAPTER 17

Tomatoes and Tomato Products

Tomatoes rank as one of the most popular items to can. Whether whole, in salsas or other sauces, or even in jams, they are a treat. Tomatoes plucked straight off the vine, still warm from the sun — there is nothing better. It's worth waiting for the season to come around, but if you can't, here are some ideas for making sure your harvest will take you (at least part of the way) through the calendar.

Q Help! Tomato overload! What is the quickest way to put 'em up?

A My favorite way to preserve tomatoes is to cold pack whole fruit, but I don't always have the time — or the patience — for the peeling and coring required. I use the recipe on page 228 when I have just that — more tomatoes than time. It's also useful when I want to process a wide variety of tomatoes. While the meaty texture of paste tomatoes makes them the best choice for cold packing, this recipe can accommodate any variety you have on hand.

Q Do I have to use plum tomatoes in my recipes?

A Plum tomatoes are the tomato of choice in many recipes. They are meaty and have relatively fewer seeds when compared to globe varieties. Globe tomatoes tend to be a bit more watery than plums, so they aren't the best choice for all recipes. You can use globe tomatoes if that is the variety you have on hand, but your recipe may have a subtler tomato flavor and be a bit looser than if you had used plum varieties.

Q Do I have to skin tomatoes before processing them?

A Skinning tomatoes is time-consuming, it's true, but most often it's a necessary part of the process. The heat of processing will separate the skins from the fruit anyway and leave you with big pieces of tough stuff floating around in your recipe, so better to get

AVALANCHE SAUCE

Makes about 3 quarts canned as juice, about 1½ quarts when reduced
to a thick sauce

*I use this recipe when the tomatoes are coming in quicker than
I can cold pack them or when I am lucky enough to have surplus
globe tomatoes on hand — the round kind that are great in recipes, but not suitable for canning whole. I can easily cook 20 to 30
pounds at a time. Now that's a workhorse of a recipe! You'll need
a food mill to process the tomatoes.*

INGREDIENTS

10 pounds tomatoes (or more), any variety, cored
      and cut into 2-inch chunks

Salt

Bottled lemon juice

PREPARE

1. Preheat the oven to 325°F.

2. Place the tomatoes in a roasting pan large enough to hold them in a single layer. Roast for 30 to 40 minutes, until the fruit is softened and no longer seeping liquid.

3. Remove from the oven and let cool slightly. Use a food mill to remove the seeds and skins, milling them directly into a large nonreactive pot that will have at least 3 to 4 inches of boiling room. Bring the purée to a boil, and then lower the heat and simmer, stirring frequently, until thickened to your desired consistency. (You may can it as is for tomato juice, reduce it by one-quarter for a thin sauce, or keep simmering until it is reduced by half for a thick sauce.) Add salt to taste.

PRESERVE

Can: Use the boiling-water method (see page 95). Add 1 tablespoon lemon juice to each pint jar and 2 tablespoons to each quart jar to be filled. Ladle the sauce into the clean, hot jars along with the lemon juice, leaving 1 inch of headspace between the top of the sauce and the lid. Use a bubble tool, or other nonmetallic implement, to release trapped air by running it along the inside of the glass. Wipe the rims, cover the jars, and screw the bands on just fingertip-tight. Process for 35 minutes for pints and 40 minutes for quarts. Turn off the heat, remove the canner lid, and let the jars rest in the water for 5 minutes. Remove the jars and set aside for 24 hours. Check seals, then store in a cool, dark place for up to 1 year.

it out of the way before you pack your jars. The only exception? You can skip the skinning, if you like, in recipes where you chop your tomatoes into small pieces, such as in salsas. Some might argue that the skins may impart a slightly bitter note to your recipe, but I've not found that to be the case. And if the skin bits are tiny enough, I don't even notice them.

Q My recipe calls for cilantro, but this herb tastes like soap to me. Are there any substitutes?

A No herb divides a crowd like cilantro. Some people love it and others can't stand it. Cilantro is an allergen for many eaters — their reaction makes the herb taste like soap — so detractors may actually be allergic to the greenery, not just picky.

You can substitute basil or parsley for cilantro, if you like. The swap will alter the flavor of the dish, but perhaps in a way that you prefer. Alternatively, you can leave out the herbs altogether. Your recipe will still taste great.

Q Why are my canned tomatoes floating to the top of the jars?

A You've got a case of *fruit float*. It is pretty common but no less distressing. Fruit float is caused by air that remains within the cell walls of the produce after processing. It happens most commonly to fruits that are canned whole or in preparations, such as quick jams, that do not cook for very long. Often, tomatoes will release this trapped air into the headspace of the sealed jar and the fruit will redistribute throughout the liquid over time. So give jars of whole tomatoes a few weeks on the shelf and they may very well turn from what looks like a failed science experiment into the gorgeous home-canned tomatoes of your dreams all on their own.

Q I have some tomatoes that are a little past their prime. Can I still preserve them?

A Tomatoes are available for such a short time each year; it seems a shame to waste a bite. Canning — either with the boiling-water method or by pressure — is recommended for tomatoes that are well ripened, though they should still be firm and nicely colored throughout. This level of ripeness ensures that they have a good pH level — essential to successful storage. And such tomatoes will keep their shape best if you can them whole.

Overripe tomatoes can be soft and will lose some of their acid as they age, making them less than ideal for canning. Any spots of mold or damage may also have increased their bacterial load beyond the carrying capacity of the canning process — a small bit of mold on the surface means that tendrils of contamination may reach down into the fruit. However, if you can trim away any damage, you can safely freeze them. While freezing will not improve the quality of the fruit, it will stop time. And while it will not eradicate contaminants, it will render mold and fungal spores inactive so they cannot do any additional damage.

To freeze the tomatoes, blanch and remove their skins (page 40) or cook down into a sauce or paste and pack into airtight containers. You needn't add citric acid or lemon juice for frozen tomatoes. They will keep in the freezer for up to 6 months.

If the tomatoes are badly rotted, their only use is in the compost bin.

Q Why do cold-packed tomatoes need to be processed for so long?

A The density of the fruit, the size of the jar, and the starting temperature of the recipe being ladled into the jar all factor into the final processing time for any product. For cold-packed tomatoes, this adds up to a processing time of well over an hour for quarts (85 minutes, to be precise). Don't cheat! It takes the heat that long to penetrate all the way to the center of the jar. Any less time and you will have an unprocessed core of food in the middle of each jar, which can lead to poor, if not dangerous, results. If you don't have the patience for the extended processing, cook your tomatoes first. Quarts of crushed, cooked tomatoes process in 45 minutes, nearly half the time.

Q There are little black spots on the lids of my tomato jars. Is this safe?

A I can't tell you how many jars of tomatoes I threw out thinking that those little spots on the lid were signs of spoilage. Such a waste. Little black spots on the *underside* of the lid of canned tomatoes are mineral deposits — they are perfectly normal and harmless. However, black spots on the top of or within the food are not okay — that is a sign of spoilage and the contents should be discarded immediately.

Q Which variety of tomato is best for canning?

A Different varieties of tomatoes are intended for different uses. You will get the best results if you choose the tomato best suited for your purpose.

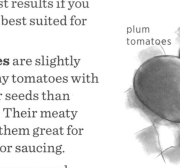

globe tomatoes

plum tomatoes

cherry tomatoes

- **Plum tomatoes** are slightly elongated, fleshy tomatoes with relatively fewer seeds than other varieties. Their meaty texture makes them great for canning whole or saucing.

- **Globe tomatoes** are much juicier than plum tomatoes and will result in a more watery product if not given the chance to cook down. Because of their high moisture content, they are not recommended for canning whole. Seeded globes are good in salsas and relishes.

- **Cherry tomatoes** are terrific eaten out of hand or halved into salads. Their high skin-to-flesh ratio makes them a challenge for processing.

Q Are heirloom tomatoes safe to can?

A Not only are they safe to can, but heirloom tomatoes are also delicious to can! Grown for their flavor rather than their ability to withstand commercial harvesting, heirloom tomatoes pack a lot of great taste. Some varieties of heirloom tomatoes are described as "low acid," which gives the impression that they may not be suitable for the canning process, but that is not the case. All tomatoes can be canned using the boiling-water method; you just have to follow your recipe.

Keep in mind that tomatoes destined for processing — by either the boiling-water method or the pressure canner — must be treated to a little boost of acid in the form of lemon juice or citric acid powder. Why? The extra acid guarantees the low pH that is necessary for safe processing using the boiling-water method, and it keeps processing times short and sweet when using a pressure canner. Whether you are canning heirloom or commercial varieties, don't leave it out!

Q I love to put lots of vegetables in my spaghetti sauce — mushrooms, peppers, onions, and even a little eggplant sometimes. Can I still can it?

A The answer is yes and no. You can can it, but since you added a lot of nonacidic ingredients to your sauce, you have to use a pressure canner. Incidentally, you have just described one of the most common mistakes that new canners make: using the boiling-water method for nonacidic recipes. While tomatoes are acidic and can be processed without pressure, adding vegetables, as you have described for this sauce, will alter the pH to a point that it is no longer suitable for the boiling-water method. Always follow your recipe. Never alter the quantity of vegetables called for or lower the amount of acid or acidic ingredients indicated; doing so could create an unstable product that can sicken you or worse. Ditto with salsas. Never add extra onions, peppers — or heaven forbid, beans — to the pot if they are not called for in your recipe.

Q I have a great recipe for marinara sauce. Can I can it?

A It depends. Did you get your recipe from a canning book? If you did, great, go right ahead and can it. If you didn't, then I would suggest you freeze your wonderful sauce rather than trying to get it shelf stable. For one thing, homemade marinara sauce often includes a fair amount of onions, garlic, and other produce that will throw off the acidic pH you need for shelf-safe products canned with the boiling-water method. Pressure canning is the preferred method for nonacidic recipes, but the timing and pressure necessary to get consistent results are impossible to determine without further testing. Stay safe: only can recipes from reliable sources.

Q Do I have to put salt in my canned tomatoes?

A Salt is frequently listed as a recommended ingredient in tomato recipes, but it is included strictly for flavor alone. The proportion of ½ teaspoon per pint jar and 1 teaspoon per quart jar will flavor your tomatoes without making them taste salty. You can add the salt to the top or bottom of the jar — it makes no difference — and the convection action of the heat through the jars will distribute it throughout. You can use less, if you prefer, or you can eliminate the salt altogether if you like.

Q I made a ton of salsa. Can I use it on anything but tortilla chips?

A You bet! Salsa is great on grilled chicken or fish. You can also blend it with some sour cream or softened cream cheese for a quick, tangy dip. Toss it with pasta for a zesty side dish. Or use it instead of sour cream and butter to top a baked potato.

Q I like fresh salsa. Do I have to cook it before I can it?

A Fresh salsa is a treat, but all recipes that are canned — whether via the boiling-water method or pressure canning — become cooked during the process. Both methods use heat to destroy any contaminating bacteria that might be lingering in the food and deactivate the enzymes that could lead to decay. So it is not possible to have fresh, canned salsa.

Q Should I use the boiling-water method or a pressure canner to can my tomatoes?

A You can use either the boiling-water method or a pressure canner to process your tomatoes. The preparation for both is the same, including acidification. For pints, use 1 tablespoon bottled lemon juice or ¼ teaspoon citric acid; double that for quarts. The boiling-water method is the easiest, but a pressure canner has a greatly reduced processing time. It's really a matter of choice and available equipment.

Q Why are tomatoes seeds sprouting in my jars?

A Germinating seeds in a canning container are an indication of spoilage. Sprouting tomato seeds are a sign that something has gone wrong, and the product should be destroyed. Possible causes include:

Insufficient processing. Tomatoes that have been processed fully will not have the enzymatic action sufficient to sprout. Always process your tomatoes for the full amount of time indicated in your recipe. If you are using the boiling-water method, be certain that during that time the water level was never less than 2 inches above the jars. If you are pressure canning, be sure that the pressure never dips lower than indicated in your recipe.

Hot storage. The cans of tomatoes may have been stored in a warm area that encouraged sprouting. Always store your jars in as dark and cool a place as possible to discourage activity within the jars.

Q I like lime juice in my salsa. Can I use that instead of vinegar?

A Lime juice is commonly added to fresh salsas to give them a citrus kick. You can sometimes find canning recipes that use citrus juices as an acidifying agent as well. If that's the case, you can certainly follow such a recipe, as long as it comes from a reliable source. Never substitute lime juice for vinegar in a recipe that doesn't call for it. Canning recipes are precisely calibrated for safe results, and you need to use the quantity and kind of acid indicated to achieve a wholesome product.

Q I like my salsas nice and thick. Can I use thickeners to give them the texture I like?

A Canned salsas have a thinner consistency than commercial brands. The extra moisture in homemade products allows the heat to penetrate to the center of the jar more easily during processing and ensures that the contents of the jar are submerged under an acidic brine during storage.

Never try to thicken your canned salsa by cooking it down or adding thickeners to the recipe. Doing so will throw off your processing time and will expose the top of your jarred ingredients during storage.

If you want a salsa that is a little thicker, drain off some of the liquid before serving. You can reserve the drained liquid and add it to soups and stews or stir it into your next Bloody Mary for a spicy kick.

Q I like my salsa extra spicy. Can I just double the amount of chiles called for in the recipe?

A You should never increase the amount of any produce ingredient in your recipe. Doing so will throw off the important acid balance that keeps your canned foods safe on the shelf and will invite contamination. You can, however, swap in hotter peppers to crank up the heat a bit. If your salsa calls for jalapeños, for example, you can substitute an equal amount of hotter chiles such as habaneros. You'll get the heat you seek without risking your results.

Q Most salsas are just too spicy for me. What can I do to temper the heat when I make them?

A One of the benefits of preserving your own food at home is that you can control the taste. If your salsa is too spicy, you can turn it down by substituting sweet peppers for a portion of the chiles called for in the recipe as long as the total weight of chiles and peppers is consistent with the recipe. For example, a salsa recipe that calls for 1 pound of chiles can be modified for milder results by using ½ pound of chiles and ½ pound of sweet bell peppers instead. Never alter the total volume of peppers in the recipe or you will throw off the acid balance necessary to keep your food safe on the shelf.

Q What are Scoville units?

A Scoville units measure the amount of capsaicin, the spicy compound found in foods such as chiles and peppercorns. The more capsaicin, the higher the number of Scoville units and the spicier the food. Jalapeño peppers, for example, are relatively mild, with a Scoville rating under 8,000 units, while the legendary ghost pepper checks in with a whopping 1,000,000 Scoville units. Hot stuff, indeed.

Q My salsa verde recipe calls for tomatillos. What are they?

A Tomatillos look like green tomatoes but are covered in a thin, papery husk that must be removed before they can be used in a recipe. Tomatillos have a tart flavor and need to be cooked to be enjoyed.

Q I just cooked up a batch of salsa and it tastes so intense. What gives?

A The flavor of canned salsas mellows over time. Right out of the pot, the vinegar might seem overwhelming and the spice level might be too strong, but give the salsa a few weeks in the jar and it will taste just right. Keep in mind, also, that hot food reveals more of its flavor than chilled bites. A spoonful of hot salsa will taste like a different recipe after it has cooled. Trust your recipe and try the salsa again after it has been processed and spent 3 to 4 weeks on the shelf.

Q Can I put black beans in my salsa?

A Even recipes that seem acidic, such as tomato sauces and salsas, do not always achieve the proper pH level necessary to be safely canned using the boiling-water method. A basic tomato sauce, for example, is a recipe that is commonly and correctly listed as safe for the boiling-water method, but the minute that recipe is altered in any way — by adding extra onions or other vegetables such as peppers or mushrooms or by adding meat to the sauce, it becomes a nonacidic recipe and must be pressure canned. The same goes for salsa. You will find many salsa recipes that are appropriate for the boiling-water method. But add extra ingredients — more peppers or a double dose of onions, or, worst of all, load it up with black beans or corn — and you will have certainly altered the pH too much for them to be canned safely with the boiling-water method.

Metric Conversions

Unless you have finely calibrated measuring equipment, conversions between U.S. and metric measurements will be somewhat inexact. It's important to convert the measurements for all of the ingredients in a recipe to maintain the same proportions as the original.

General Formulas	
Ounces to grams	multiply ounces by 28.35
Grams to ounces	multiply grams by 0.035
Pounds to grams	multiply pounds by 453.5
Pounds to kilograms	multiply pounds by 0.45
Cups to liters	multiply cups by 0.24
Fahrenheit to Celsius	subtract 32 from Fahrenheit temperature, multiply by 5, then divide by 9
Celsius to Fahrenheit	multiply Celsius temperature by 9, divide by 5, then add 32

Approximate Equivalents by Weight	
U.S.	**Metric**
¼ ounce	7 grams
½ ounce	14 grams
1 ounce	28 grams
1¼ ounces	35 grams
1½ ounces	40 grams
2½ ounces	70 grams
4 ounces	112 grams
5 ounces	140 grams
8 ounces	228 grams
10 ounces	280 grams
15 ounces	425 grams
16 ounces (1 pound)	454 grams
0.035 ounces	1 gram
1.75 ounces	50 grams
3.5 ounces	100 grams
8.75 ounces	250 grams
1.1 pounds	500 grams
2.2 pounds	1 kilogram

Approximate Equivalents by Volume	
U.S.	**Metric**
1 teaspoon	5 milliliters
1 tablespoon	15 milliliters
¼ cup	60 milliliters
½ cup	120 milliliters
1 cup	230 milliliters
1¼ cups	300 milliliters
1½ cups	360 milliliters
2 cups	460 milliliters
2½ cups	600 milliliters
3 cups	700 milliliters
4 cups (1 quart)	0.95 liter
1.06 quarts	1 liter
4 quarts (1 gallon)	3.8 liters

Resources

A few key pieces of equipment and delicious ingredients are all you need to preserve your own food. Here are some resources to help you get your hands on everything you need to put 'em up!

Supplies and Equipment

Your local hardware store probably has all that you need to preserve your own food. Shopping at local, independent retailers is a great way to keep dollars in your community. If you don't have a store close to you or are having trouble getting what you need, these sites are great resources. Many also offer steep discounts for bulk orders, so if you are canning with a group, some may be able to help you with volume discounts.

Canning Pantry
800-285-9044
www.canningpantry.com

Canning Pantry is a quaint online store that caters to the home food preserving community. A good source for pectin and citric acid as well as other items.

Fresh Preserving
Jarden Home Brands
800-240-3340
www.freshpreserving.com

Fresh Preserving is Ball's online resource for tips and equipment. You can order jars and more from them directly through this website. They carry exclusively their own brand.

Goodman's
888-333-4660
www.goodmans.net

Goodman's carries a large selection of canning supplies. They also offer jars in large quantity at discount prices.

Kitchen Krafts, Inc.
800-298-5389
www.kitchenkrafts.com

Kitchen Krafts offers a large selection of products for unique kitchen projects. They have a full line of supplies and equipment for home preservers.

Lehman's
888-438-5346
www.lehmans.com

Lehman's offers a wide range of home supplies, including everything you need for home food preservation. A great resource for buying supplies in bulk.

Pomona's Universal Pectin

www.pomonapectin.com

Home of Pomona's Universal Pectin, this website is dedicated exclusively to this product. You can source the pectin and get more information about it here.

Tattler Reusable Canning Lids

S&S Innovations Corp.
877-747-2793
www.reusablecanninglids.com

This site offers Tattler's reusable lids, replacement gaskets, and fresh rings.

Home Food Preserving Community and Information

There is a lot of misguided information on the Internet about everything, home food preservation included. If you are going to use online resources for info about food preservation, it is critical that you glean your info from a reliable source. The websites listed in this chapter are top-notch. They are published by folks who know their stuff, so you will get delicious, safe results with their tips, tricks, and recipes.

Canning Across America

www.canningacrossamerica.com

A lovely group of canners dedicated to spreading the good word about this nifty craft. Visit their website for recipes and giveaways and to keep up to date with their national and local events.

Edible Communities, Inc.

www.ediblecommunities.com

A national network of locally produced publications, Edible Communities can put you in touch with your local food community like no one else.

Food in Jars

www.foodinjars.com

Marisa McClellan's blog is always fresh and populated with great ideas for canning and preserving.

National Center for Home Food Preservation

http://nchfp.uga.edu

This website, funded in part by the USDA, offers information and recipes that are thoroughly tested for safe and successful results.

Mother Earth News

www.motherearthnews.com

Trust your Mother! There's a reason why this is one of the oldest and most well-regarded resources for sustainable living. The site, as well as the printed magazine, is full of good, useful information.

PickYourOwn.org

www.pickyourown.org

This is a sweet, homespun site that is chock-full of great information on home food preservation and local sourcing. A great resource for farmers and those who love them.

Punk Domestics
www.punkdomestics.com

Punk Domestics is a rich resource for deep DIY food craft. Canning, fermenting, charcuterie, even beer and wine making are covered on this site of community-sourced information.

Wild Fermentation
www.wildfermentation.com

A rich website from the father of the ferment, Sandor Katz. This is the quintessential source for fermentation information.

Local Food Sources and Calendars

Local food is delicious food, and it's the best choice when you are preserving. These websites can help you find locally produced foods in your area.

Alabama
Availability Chart
Farmers Market Authority
www.fma.alabama.gov/avail_chart.htm

Alaska
Division of Agriculture
Alaska Department of Natural Resources
http://dnr.alaska.gov/ag

Arizona
Fill Your Plate
Arizona Farm Bureau
http://fillyourplate.org/produce-season.html

Arkansas
Arkansas Grown
www.arkansasgrown.org

California
Bay Area
Center for Urban Education about Sustainable Agriculture
www.cuesa.org

Southern California
Sustainable Economic Enterprises of Los Angeles
www.farmernet.com

Colorado
Colorado Farmers Market Association
www.coloradofarmers.org

Connecticut
buyCTgrown
http://buyctgrown.com

Delaware
Delaware Farmers' Markets
Delaware Department of Agriculture
http://dda.delaware.gov/marketing/delaware_farmers_markets.shtml

District of Columbia
Calendar of Maryland Harvests
Maryland Manual, Agriculture
www.msa.md.gov/msa/mdmanual/01glance/html/agripro.html

Florida
Florida Crops and Products
Florida Department of Agriculture and Consumer Services
http://florida-agriculture.com/consumers/crops/inseason/

Georgia
Georgia Harvest Calendar
Georgia Farm Bureau
www.gfb.org/commodities/cfm/harvest_calendar.html

Hawaii
Department of Agriculture
hawaii.gov/hdoa/add/farmers-market-in-hawaii/farmers-market-listing

Idaho
Idaho Preferred
Idaho Department of Agriculture
http://idahopreferred.com

Illinois
Farmers Markets
Bureau of Marketing and Promotions
www.agr.state.il.us/markets/farmers

Indiana
Indiana MarketMaker
www.in.gov/isda/2342.htm

Iowa
Produce Availability Calendar
Horticulture and Farmers Market Bureau
www.iowaagriculture.gov/horticulture_and_farmersmarkets/harvestcalendar.asp

Kansas
Kansas Farmers Markets
www.ksfarmersmarkets.org

Kentucky
Farmers' Market
Kentucky Department of Agriculture
www.kyagr.com/marketing/farmers-market.html

Louisiana
Louisiana Grown
www.louisianagrown.com

Maine
Get Real. Get Maine!
Maine Department of Agriculture
www.getrealmaine.com

Maryland
Maryland's Best
Maryland Department of Agriculture
http://marylandsbest.net

Massachusetts
Mass Farmers Markets
www.massfarmersmarkets.org

Michigan
Michigan Farmers Market Association
http://mifma.org

Minnesota
Minnesota Grown
Minnesota Department of Agriculture
www3.mda.state.mn.us/mngrown

Mississippi

Mississippi Farmers Market
Mississippi Department of
Agriculture & Commerce
www.mdac.state.ms.us/
departments/ms_farmers_
market/index.html

Missouri

**Missouri Farmers' Market
Directory**
Missouri Department of
Agriculture
http://agebb.missouri.edu/fmktdir

Montana

Farmers Markets
Montana Department of
Agriculture
http://agr.mt.gov/agr/Programs/
FarmersMarkets

Nebraska

**Nebraska Produce Availability
Chart**
Nebraska Our Best to You
www.ourbesttoyou.nebraska.gov/
harvest_calendar.html

Nevada

Nevada Grown
http://nevadagrown.com

New Hampshire

**New Hampshire Farmer's Market
Association**
www.nhfma.org

New Jersey

**New Jersey Farmers' Market
Council of Farmers and
Communities**
www.jerseyfarmersmarkets.com

New Mexico

**New Mexico Farmers' Marketing
Association**
www.farmersmarketsnm.org

New York

**New York State
Farmers Market Federation of
New York**
www.nyfarmersmarket.com
**New York City
GrowNYC**
www.growny.org

North Carolina

North Carolina Farm Fresh
www.ncfarmfresh.com

North Dakota

Farmers Markets
North Dakota Department of
Agriculture
www.nd.gov/ndda/program/
farmers-markets

Ohio

Ohio Proud
www.ohioproud.com

Oklahoma

OK Grown
www.okgrown.com

Oregon

**Oregon Farmer's Markets
Association**
www.oregonfarmersmarkets.org

Pennsylvania

Pennsylvania Buy Fresh Buy Local
www.buylocalpa.org

Rhode Island

Farm Fresh Rhode Island
www.farmfreshri.org

South Carolina
**Caroline Farm Stewardship
Association**
www.carolinafarmstewards.org

South Dakota
**South Dakota Local Foods
Directory**
www.sdlocalfoods.org

Tennessee
**Pick Tennessee Products
Tennessee Department of
Agriculture Market Development
Division**
http://picktnproducts.org

Texas
**Certified Farmers Markets
Texas Department of Agriculture**
http://gotexan.org/
LocateGOTEXAN/
CertifiedFarmersMarkets.aspx

Utah
Utah's Own
http://utahsown.utah.gov

Vermont
**Farmers' Market Directory
Northeast Organic Farming
Association of Vermont**
http://nofavt.org/
find-organic-food/
farmers-market-directory

Virginia
**Virginia Grown
Virginia Department of
Agriculture and Consumer
Services**
www.vdacs.virginia.gov/vagrown

Washington
**Washington State Farmers Market
Association**
www.wafarmersmarkets.com

West Virginia
**West Virginia Farmers Market
Association**
www.wvfarmers.org

Wisconsin
**Wisconsin Farmers Markets
AnythingWisconsin.com**
www.anythingwisconsin.com/
farmmarkets.htm

Wyoming
**Wyoming Farmers Marketing
Association**
www.wyomingfarmersmarkets.org

Index

Page numbers in *italics* indicate illustrations. Page numbers in **bold** indicate tables.

246